COLLEGE OF ALA
WITHDRAWN

Coping with

DYSLEXIA

Karen Donnelly

The Rosen Publishing Group, Inc.
New York

Published in 2000 by The Rosen Publishing Group, Inc.
29 East 21st Street, New York, NY 10010

Cover photo by Michelle Edwards

First Edition

Library of Congress Cataloging-in-Publication Data

Donnelly, Karen.
    Coping with dyslexia / by Karen Donnelly.—1st ed.
    p. cm.
    Includes bibliographical references and index.
    ISBN 0-8239-2850-0 (library binding)
    1. Dyslexia—Juvenile literature. [1. Dyslexia.] I. Title.

RJ496.A5 D66 2000
616.85'53—dc21   00-009278

About the Author

Karen Donnelly has a master's degree in English literature from Southern Connecticut State University. She has written numerous books and newspaper and magazine articles for children and adults on topics such as nature, architecture, careers, and health. She lives in Connecticut with her husband, David, and their daughters, Colleen and Cathy.

Acknowledgments

This book is dedicated to the children and adults who struggle every day with undiagnosed learning differences. It is also dedicated to the teachers who have taken the time to help dyslexic students compensate for those differences, and to the parents who share the frustrations of those students. Finally, it is dedicated to Charles and Helen Schwab, founders of The Schwab Foundation for Learning, a powerful tool in helping children with learning difficulties.

Contents

Learning the Hard Way

Charles R. Schwab founded his brokerage firm, Charles Schwab & Co., in 1971. Today, this company is one of America's largest brokerage firms, with 270 offices around the country. But his success has not come easily. Charles Schwab is dyslexic, a difference he did not understand until his eight-year-old son began having reading difficulties.

When his son's dyslexia was diagnosed, Charles's own struggle with reading and spelling finally made sense. Dyslexia often runs in families. Charles realized that he must also be dyslexic. Having a name for his son's condition did not make things easier. Very little information was available. Charles and his wife, Helen, always wondered whether they were making the best choices for their son.

Charles and Helen wanted other parents with dyslexic children to have an easier time finding the information they need. The Schwabs founded the Schwab Foundation for Learning in 1987. The foundation provides services and support to parents and students with learning differences. It also supports projects that help families learn about learning differences and find the resources they need.

In addition to helping their son and children like him compensate for their learning difference, the Schwabs understand how important it is to maintain self-esteem. "That's the real problem with learning differences," explains Charles. "Some kids feel like they're stupid. I want them to know that they're not. They just learn differently. Once they understand that and have the tools to compensate, then they can feel good about themselves."

Charles Schwab's dyslexia did not stop him. He earned bachelor and graduate degrees from Stanford University. In fact, Charles credits much of his success to his learning style and the vision it affords him.

Nothing to Fear

Nothing in life is to be feared. It is only to be understood.
Marie Curie, scientist and discoverer
of the element radium

Dyslexia is a learning disability. People with dyslexia usually have difficulty reading. So, you may ask, what good is a book about coping with dyslexia going to do a person who may not be able to read it?

That is a good question. One answer is, a person who is dyslexic is not the only one coping with his or her condition. Parents, teacher, counselors, and friends all need help understanding the struggle and hard work that fill a large part of a dyslexic person's day. They need to recognize that laziness or lack of intelligence does not cause dyslexia. The more they understand about how dyslexics learn, the better.

Furthermore, this book *is* useful for people who are dyslexic. They may need help understanding some of the words. But the people who help them are probably also interested in understanding their condition. The educational resources, study suggestions, college and employment information, and legal rights are all important for a dyslexic student considering his or her future path.

Finally, the information contained in this book is important for all of us. Nearly 15 percent of Americans struggle with learning disabilities. A greater understanding of people with dyslexia will make the differences seem smaller and the similarities more important.

The causes of dyslexia still remain a mystery. As a result, educators and researchers disagree about the best ways to help dyslexics learn. The resources and information found in this book are intended to guide dyslexics as they search for what best fits their needs. According to research studies, almost all parents surveyed would seek medical help if a child were identified with a learning disability. Most would go to their doctor. Others would look to their school administration or their child's teacher. Unfortunately, these sources are often poorly prepared to help. As a result, dyslexic students and their parents must become self-advocates. This book does not endorse or recommend one resource over another. Only you and your parents can determine what will work best for you.

In the early 1990s, I was teaching English 99 at a local community college. English 99 was a remedial course, reinforcing the basics of grammar to students who tested below college level. My class was a mixture of recent high school graduates and adults returning to college. For many, English was their second language.

During the semester, one of my students, Nico (not his real name), began to stand out. It became clear to me that Nico could not read. I was very angry—not at Nico, but at a school system that would pass him from grade to grade. I was horrified that he had graduated from high school but none of his teachers had taught him to read. He could not spell. His handwriting was terrible.

I suggested to Nico that he go to the Office of Support Services and sign up with a tutor. In reality, though, I knew that the level of Nico's skills was so below average that the help he would get from a student tutor would probably not be enough.

Nico came to class for about a month. During that time, I stopped asking him to read his homework assignment out loud. I thought I was sparing him embarrassment. He received D's and F's on his papers. I asked him several times if he had gotten a tutor. He usually just shrugged his shoulders.

Eventually, Nico stopped coming to class. I lost track of him. At the end of the semester, I gave him a grade of "N," which meant that he had been listed on the class roster but had never attended class. I didn't want him to have an F on his permanent record.

I know now that Nico is dyslexic. At the time, I knew nothing about dyslexia. I had a master's degree in English literature but was not trained to recognize learning differences. I felt badly for Nico. I was angry at a system that had failed him. Then I became part of the same system. I failed him, too. The memory of Nico still haunts me.

According to a report by the National Adult Literacy and Learning Disabilities Center, 60 percent of adults with severe literacy problems have undetected and/or untreated learning disabilities.

Dyslexia: Not a Disease

The biggest help for dyslexic kids is to convince them it's not their fault.
Robert Rauschenberg, dyslexic and famous artist

Dyslexia is not a disease; it is a condition you are born with. You cannot "catch" it. It will not go away. Probably someone else in your family, maybe your father or a cousin, also has it. Boys are affected three to six times more frequently than girls are.

When this condition was first identified in 1876, it was called "word blindness." The word we use today, dyslexia, comes from the Greek words *dys* (meaning poor) and *lexis* (meaning word or language). Dyslexia is considered a learning disability not because people who have it are less intelligent, but because they understand words and language differently than others do. This gap in understanding means that to teach dyslexics how to use language, we need to use different methods.

Studying dyslexia has proven difficult for educators and researchers because they cannot "see" how dyslexics process words and letters. Imagine, for example, that your brain was unable to recognize the color red. When you looked at a rose, it appeared green. How would you explain what you saw to someone whose brain could not recognize green but "saw" only red? Would you be able to describe what "green" is to someone who has never seen it? A similar gap in understanding exists between those who are dyslexic and those who are not.

This gap has narrowed, however, as researchers and dyslexics work together to find ways to understand each other. Scientists have some information about how most people understand language. They need to use that knowledge to help them understand the different ways language is processed by dyslexics.

Language is made up of symbols. A language symbol has three parts: what it looks like, what it means, and what it sounds like. When most people read silently, they "hear" the sounds of the words and "listen" to the sentences in their heads.

If you are dyslexic, you may not have this internal voice in your head. You think in pictures. When you see a word, your brain "sees" a picture. As long as the word means a "real" thing, like *dog* or *apple*, you can form that picture. Verbs that describe real action can also be formed into pictures, like *run* or *cry*. You have seen these actions happen, so you know what they are. The biggest problem for dyslexics is often caused by words that cannot be formed into pictures. Unfortunately, these words occur often, and without them, sentences break down. Words like the, *a, an, there, is, are, was, were,* and even *and* create confusion and disorientation for dyslexics.

Ronald B. Davis, author of *The Gift of Dyslexia,* is also dyslexic. He calls these words "trigger words." In his book, he gives the example of a ten-year-old boy trying to read. A sentence that would be simple for a child who thinks with the sounds of the words is very difficult for a dyslexic boy. Here is the sentence:

> *The brown horse jumped over the stone fence and ran through the pasture.*

Immediately, the first word causes confusion. The boy passes over it. He looks at the word *brown* and makes a mental picture of the color brown. The word *horse* gives shape to the brown color. The boy now has a picture of a brown horse. The words *jumped over* cause the horse to rise into the air. The word *the* again causes blankness and confusion. *Stone* gives a picture of a rock, and *fence* a picture of a fence. So far, the boy has a jumping brown horse and a rock fence, and he is trying to make some meaning from them. When he reaches the word *and,* he skips it. He sees the word *ran* and pictures himself running, an image totally unconnected to the horse. He changes the word *through* into *throw* in his mind. He sees himself throwing a ball. He skips the word *the.* The word *pasture* must be decoded one letter at a time. "When asked what he just read, he is likely to answer with something like 'a place where grass grows,'" wrote Davis. "The boy has a picture of a horse in the air, a stone fence, himself playing ball, and a grassy place, but cannot relate the separate pieces of the sentence to form a mental image of the scene described." He may realize that he has not understood what he read. He may try reading the sentence again. But without new skills, the result will probably be the same.

The English language is especially difficult for dyslexics. So many words sound alike but are spelled differently.

Silent letters make spelling a nightmare. Why do *shoe* and *show* sound different? How can *through* and *threw* have the same sound? Why doesn't *toe* rhyme with *shoe*? Why does it need that extra *e* on the end? How can anyone EVER understand how to pronounce the word *thigh*?

There are several theories about how best to teach dyslexics to understand and use language. Because each student is different, no one method can be determined to be the only correct one. Teachers, parents and students must work together to find what works best for each individual.

One thing is certain. Dyslexia is NOT a result of laziness, lack of motivation, sensory deprivation, poor education, environmental conditions, or low intelligence.

Characteristics of Dyslexia

Reading before the class was the most frustrating thing for me . . . I felt like I was dumb. I was really embarrassed.

Tom Cruise, movie star and dyslexic

Brian's family had moved around a lot. From first to sixth grade, he went to four different schools. In fourth grade, he even had to start a new school in the middle of the year. What a nightmare that was!

When Brian walked into his fourth-grade classroom for the first time, his new teacher, Ms. Walker, introduced him to the class. "Boys and girls, this is Brian. He just moved to Bridgewater. He will be in our class," she said. Then she turned to Brian. "Brian, will you please write your name on the blackboard? That will help us all remember it."

Brian's palms began to sweat. He turned toward the blackboard and picked up a piece of chalk. He took a deep breath and began to write: B-r-a-i-n.

"Brain. His name is Brain!" The students were pointing and laughing. Brian could feel his eyes filling with tears. He was afraid to turn around. He did not want the other kids to see him crying.

Ms. Walker put her hand on Brian's shoulder. "I am sorry, Brian," she whispered. To the class she said, "That is very good, class. I am glad you found that spelling error so quickly. Thank you for helping us with our language lesson today, Brian."

"Now, Amy, will you please come to the board and write the sentence: Bobby said on the way to the store I lost my way. Leave out all the punctuation. Class, see if you can do as well with this sentence as you did with one word."

"Brian will sit at the desk next to you, Montell," Ms. Walker said. "But before he sits down, will you please show him where the boys' bathroom is?"

"Sure," said Montell.

Brian took a deep breath and followed Montell into the hall. Brian thought that this had to be the worst day of his life.

According to the National Institutes of Health, nearly 15 percent of Americans are challenged by a learning disability, including about 2.4 million schoolchildren. People with dyslexia are not all the same, which sometimes makes diagnosis difficult. The condition affects different people in different ways. These are some of the most common signs:

1. Difficulty identifying individual words—for example, confusing *because* with *become.*

2. Difficulty identifying separate phonetic sounds in words.

3. Difficulty identifying sequences of sounds in syllables and sentences.

4. Difficulty spelling.

5. Mixing up or reversing numbers and letters when reading or writing—for example *b* for *d,* 52 for 25, or *left* for *felt.*

6. Delayed spoken language.

7. Problems remembering what is read.

8. Difficulty expressing thoughts in writing or while speaking.

9. Difficulty completely understanding instructions that are heard.

10. Confusing direction—for example, right and left.

11. Confusing space—for example, up and down.

12. Confusing time—for example, yesterday and tomorrow.

13. Confusing right- or left-handedness.

14. Illegible handwriting.

15. Difficulty with mathematics, especially math problems involving sequences of steps.

Individuals with dyslexia most likely do not have all of these conditions. This is one reason dyslexia can be difficult to diagnose. If you believe it is possible that you are dyslexic, you should arrange for an evaluation as soon as possible. The test results will help you, your family, and your teachers understand the problem more clearly. Test results can also make you eligible for special education services. You may also be eligible for special testing accommodations and programs that may be offered by colleges and universities. The test results will provide the basis from which teachers and counselors will make recommendations for your educational program. They will also provide guidelines for continued evaluation of that program.

Dyslexia is a condition you are born with. That means that your brain has been "seeing" the information it receives differently from the time you were born. This difference probably did not become a cause for concern until you entered elementary school. In kindergarten, you may have had difficulty learning the alphabet. But the differences began to cause the biggest problems as you and your friends began to read. The words did not make sense to you. They seemed to jump and jumble all over the page. You had great ideas in your head, but for some reason were unable to put them down on paper. You may have started to think you were stupid because even when you thought you knew the answers, you received poor grades on your tests.

The earlier that dyslexia is discovered, the sooner educational intervention can begin. That means that programs can be developed to help you better understand the way language works and to help you learn how to live with your dyslexia.

What Causes Dyslexia?

I remember I used to never be able to get along at school. I was always at the foot of the class . . . my father thought I was stupid, and I almost decided that I was a dunce.
Thomas Alva Edison, scientist, inventor, and dyslexic

Researchers are still struggling to uncover the cause of dyslexia. Several theories are being studied. Recent research by Dr. Sally Shaywitz, a professor of pediatrics at Yale University School of Medicine, indicates that dyslexia is caused by a functional disruption in the brain. Dr. Shaywitz uses a technology called functional magnetic resonance imaging (FMRI) that allows her to look into the brain while it is working. During one of her studies, she watched the brains of thirty-two non-dyslexic adults and twenty-nine dyslexic adults while they worked on tasks that involved language. Her findings were published in the 1998 *Proceedings of the National Academy of Sciences.* They showed that the activity patterns in the area of the brain responsible for reading in dyslexic readers differed from those of nondyslexic readers. The new images showed that nondyslexic readers increased their brain activity when the tasks became more difficult. The brain activity of dyslexics did not increase. These results indicate that a neurological basis for dyslexia does exist.

Since the 1970s, Dr. Harold Levinson has contended that dyslexia is the result of an inner-ear disturbance. In his original study, published in the 1973 *Journal of the American Academy of Child Psychiatry*, Dr. Levinson stated that over 96 percent of the dyslexics tested for the study had a malfunction of the inner ear. Dr. Levinson theorizes that this malfunction causes signals to the brain to be "scrambled." The brain cannot process, or "read," these scrambled signals, and the confusion results in dyslexic symptoms. The severity of dyslexic symptoms depends on the degree of signal scrambling.

Dr. Levinson believes that dyslexia is a medical problem and should be treated as such. Medical testing to measure hearing, balance and coordination, and eye movement—all functions related to the inner ear—is recommended, along with neurological testing. By correcting the inner-ear malfunction, usually with medication, the scrambled signals will be reduced. Dr. Levinson's treatments include motion-sickness medication to improve balance. Nutritional treatments using niacin, related B vitamins, and other minerals may be recommended.

Dr. Levinson believes that, while analyzing the brain functions of dyslexics, traditional researchers have interpreted their data incorrectly. He does not disagree that the brain function of dyslexics is different from those who are not dyslexic. He believes, however, that this difference is not the cause of dyslexia, but the result. The scrambled signals received by a malfunctioning inner-ear cause the brain to respond differently than it would if the signals were "normal." "If dyslexics versus 'normals' send scrambled signals to their thinking brains," Dr. Levinson wrote, "isn't it reasonable to assume that a normal thinking brain, via compensatory adaptations, will handle these abnormal versus normal signals differently?"

Dr. Levinson's research and suggested treatments are controversial. His ideas are not shared by the many educators and scientists he calls "traditionalists." These traditionalists include those who follow the Orton-Gillingham program, the most common method of teaching dyslexics.

Other Language Difficulties

Dyslexics have difficulty reading. But their language differences can cause other struggles, too.

Dysgraphia

Every morning, Michael's social studies teacher, Ms. Burke, wrote a homework assignment on the blackboard. As the students came into the classroom, they were expected to quickly copy the assignment. For his classmates, this was a simple task. But not for Michael.

That morning's assignment was to read chapter 8, pages 114–123, and answer the questions for discussion that followed the chapter.

Earlier in the school year, Michael had dreaded coming to social studies. He could not copy the assignment fast enough. When he took his eyes off his paper to look up at the blackboard, his pen seemed to move as if it had a mind of its own. He had trouble putting the point back in the right place. The letters wandered over the paper. He gripped the pen so hard his hands hurt.

When he got home and looked at what he had written, it made no sense. Even his mother could not understand the small, cramped writing. Michael tried to remember the assignment but usually got it wrong.

One day, Michael's mom, Margaret, suggested a solution.

"I will call Ms. Burke and see if we can speak with her after school, okay?" said Margaret.

"Okay," said Michael. "I guess things can't get any worse."

Ms. Burke agreed to a meeting.

"I know that you ask your students to copy their homework assignment from the blackboard," said Margaret. "But did you know that Michael is dysgraphic?"

"I am not sure what that means," said Ms. Burke.

"It means that he has difficulty writing. His writing looks sloppy, but it is not because he is lazy or does not care," said Margaret. "He has trouble coordinating his hand and the pen on the paper, especially if he has to look up to the blackboard to copy something."

"That is why I keep messing up my homework assignments," said Michael. "When I get home, I can't figure out what I wrote. Half the time, I did not finish copying the assignment."

"I did not realize you had this difficulty," said Ms. Burke. "Do you have a solution?"

"I would like to ask that Michael bring a tape recorder to class," said Margaret. "He could read the assignment into the recorder. Then Michael can play it back at home. Michael remembers what he hears very well. He may not even need the tape recorder. But it will be a good way to check that he remembers correctly."

Since the meeting, Michael has done much better in his social studies class. Ms. Burke also suggested that Michael use his tape recorder when she lectured. Michael did not take notes before, but now he could use the taped lectures to help him remember what he heard. Ms. Burke also let him talk into the recorder to answer essay questions on her tests. Michael's grade went from D to B. He always knew most of the answers. He just was not able to write them down fast enough.

Many dyslexics find handwriting difficult. This is called dyslexic dysgraphia. It is true, of course, that many people who are not dyslexic have very poor handwriting. Doctors are famous for having illegible signatures. People with poor handwriting are not necessarily dysgraphic.

People with dysgraphia have poor handwriting, but not because they are careless or sloppy. Instead, they experience real difficulty in transferring the image of the letter or word that they "see" in their brain to a piece of paper. This process becomes especially difficult if they are asked to look at a word and copy it from something else, like a blackboard, to their paper. Copying notes from the blackboard can be a stressful, or even painful, chore for someone with dysgraphia.

If you are dysgraphic, your writing may seem to wander up and down on the page. The task of placing the pencil in the correct spot after each letter is completed may be so difficult that it sometimes causes you to forget what you were planning to write. Letters are often very small. Words may be a mixture of upper and lower case letters. Writing takes a long time and is very tiring.

For most students, copying assignments or notes from the blackboard is a simple process. So the extra time and effort required by dysgraphic students is painfully obvious. In elementary school, you may have been forced to give up recess to finish. Maybe you needed to take home assignments that should have been completed in class. This added to your homework volume and the time that you needed to complete it. Your teachers may have insisted that you recopy your work. Unfortunately, the second attempt was probably not better.

This painful struggle to complete what other students find a simple task can cause stress and emotional problems. Your classmates may have laughed at you. Simply looking at a writing sample is not enough to diagnose dysgraphia. A qualified individual must observe you while you are writing. The tester will consider your posture, pencil grip, and stress level in addition to the finished sample.

Educators have not yet agreed upon the best method for correcting dysgraphia. The Orton-Gillingham method recommends slow, repetitious practice beginning with individual letters. Students and their parents must investigate all options and decide what will work best.

Sometimes, changing the writing tool or using pencil grips may prove helpful. Your teacher may let you use a tape recorder. If teachers are using their own notes to copy onto the board, they may be willing to provide a photocopy of those notes to you.

The computer may be the best tool against dysgraphia. Word-processing programs eliminate the need to actually form letters. Spell-checking tools can help correct substituted or reversed letters.

Spelling Difficulties

Lots of very intelligent people are poor spellers. The English language sometimes seems to be designed to make spelling difficult. Many words combine letters in ways that have nothing to do with the phonetic sounds we assign to them. Words like *foreign, maneuver,* and *delicious* all contain letter combinations that cannot easily be sounded out. The spelling of common words like *does, they, come, though,* and *through* seem to have no relationship to the way they are pronounced. Homonyms, words that sound the same but are spelled differently, like *there/their, dye/die,* and *sun/son* can cause nightmares. Every spelling rule has exceptions.

Most students learn, at least in part, to spell by sound, or phonetically. They hear the sound of the word in their heads when they read and are able to spell it based on those sounds. Even the "whole language" approach, which teaches reading and spelling based on whole-word recognition, needs some phonetics.

According to Ronald Davis, author of *The Gift of Dyslexia,* dyslexic students do not hear those "head sounds." They must memorize letter-sound associations. The Orton-Gillingham multisensory teaching system recommends that dyslexic students practice writing words correctly. Those who support this system believe that by writing words over and over, dyslexic students will learn to spell them correctly. They also recommend memorizing a few "sight" words that students will recognize as a whole. Each dyslexic student and his or her parents must search for the method that works best for them.

Multisensory
Teaching

One of the most common methods of teaching people with dyslexia is called multisensory teaching. Students learn to link a sound to a written letter. They also learn to connect that sound and the way the written letter looks with the way it feels to write the letter. This is a slow process and requires a great deal of patience and practice.

Multisensory techniques were first used by Dr. Samuel Orton in the 1920s. Dr. Orton was influenced by the "tactile" method of teaching, learning by feel or touch, described by Helen Keller. Using this method, students are taught to use different patterns to write letters that may be easily confused. Many dyslexic students, for example, reverse *b* and *d*. They are taught to use different strokes to write each letter. When printing the letter *b*, they make the vertical line first and the circle second. When printing a *d*, they make the circle first and then draw the line. Anna Gillingham and Bessie Stillman expanded the multisensory approach in 1936. Today, the Orton-Gillingham approach combines the multisensory techniques originated by Orton and Gillingham.

The International Dyslexia Association (formerly the Orton Dyslexia Society) asserts that "when taught by a multisensory approach, learners have the advantage of learning alphabetic patterns and words by utilizing three pathways." Multisensory approaches teach direct letter-sound relationships, syllable patterns, and the meaning of word parts. Multisensory teaching includes these parts:

Phonology and Phonological Awareness: Phonology is the study of sounds and how they work. Phonological awareness means the understanding of how sounds work in words. It is the ability to break words down into the sounds that form them.

Sound-Symbol Awareness: Sound-symbol awareness means understanding how a symbol, like a letter or combination of letters, relates to a sound. What sound does *b* or *ch* make? First a student is taught what sound goes with each letter. Then he or she is taught to understand the sounds made by letter blends, like *ch*, *br*, or *str*. This awareness should let a student reverse the process and break down a word into its individual sounds.

Syllable Instruction: A syllable is a part of a word with one vowel sound. This part of the multisensory approach teaches the six basic types of syllables and the rules for dividing words into syllables.

Morphology: Morphology is the study of how parts join to form a word. These parts include prefixes, suffixes, roots, and base words.

Syntax: Understanding syntax lets students use words to build sentences. Teaching syntax shows students how the order of words creates meaning. Grammar and different kinds of sentence structures are important parts of syntax.

Semantics: Semantics is meaning. Students are taught how to understand language as a whole.

The Orton-Gillingham approach takes students from the smallest piece of language, a single letter, through groups of letters, to syllables, words, sentences, and groups of sentences. It is taught using all learning pathways: sight, sound, and tactile (touch) stimulation. Because each student will respond differently to stimulation, using all pathways should increase the possibility of success. Teaching should follow the logical order of learning language. The smallest and easiest parts should be taught first. Additional steps will be based on skills already learned. All skills should be practiced and reinforced.

Many variations of the Orton-Gillingham approach have been developed as researchers and teachers study the needs and successes of students with dyslexia. Most involve some or all of these teaching strategies:

1. Teach students to understand how speech and sound work with letter combinations. How does *ch* sound? How do you spell the word *church* which begins and ends with this sound?

2. Teach students how the alphabet works. Begin with individual letters and move to combinations of letters. How can you break down a combination of letters into sounds?

3. When asking the student to read, use books that include many words that the student knows. Using books that include many words the student

cannot read will frustrate the student. Most likely, rather than actually decoding the word, the student will often guess.

4. Reinforce words that the student knows until they become automatic. Add to this vocabulary so that more and more words are at the student's fingertips.

5. Teach parts of a story. What makes up a story? Character, setting, and conflict. Teach the student to look for these parts to help them understand and remember the action of the story.

6. Teach children the relationship between spelling and reading. Help them understand that spelling words correctly will help them communicate with others in writing.

7. Review and practice.

8. Practice and review.

9. Review and practice again.

The Social Strain
of Dyslexia

You are dyslexic. That does not mean you are stupid. Having dyslexia means you are different—not better or worse than other kids, just different.

But sometimes, especially in adolescence, being different can be the worst thing in the world. For teenagers, fitting in with peers is very important. While social acceptance leaves room for a bit of individuality, most kids want to be just like everyone else. Clothing, hairstyles, and makeup are usually chosen based on what is currently popular. You probably act in a way that you believe will make you part of the group. Most teenagers do not want to be outsiders.

Being dyslexic makes you different. So even though other people tell you that you should not feel badly about it, chances are you do, at least some of the time. Your parents may be very supportive, but they cannot go to school with you. You have to work out your social anxieties and find a way to fit in at your school. Your social difficulties may be even harder for you to overcome than your learning differences.

The way you act about your dyslexia will set the tone for how others act toward you. If you seem embarrassed about your learning difficulties, other students will be more likely to act as if you should be embarrassed.

Kids can be really mean. You do not have to be dyslexic to find that out. If you look around you and pay attention, you will find that most of your fellow students are dealing with social rejection at least some of the time. You need to decide how you will let rejection affect you.

Not everyone will be your friend. That would be true even if you were not dyslexic. But you do need at least one friend whom you can count on. Your counselor may be able to help you find a support group in your area. Talking to other students with dyslexia may help relieve some of your frustrations.

The level of your social anxiety may be related to how early your dyslexia was diagnosed. If it was discovered early in grade school, you probably have developed coping skills and built friendships. But if your dyslexia went undiagnosed for years, your social problems are probably greater. You may have been forced to repeat a grade. You may have felt stupid because other students found learning so much easier. You may have been left behind as they worked in class.

If a teacher recognized your dyslexia, he or she probably referred you to a counselor. But many teachers are not trained to recognize learning disabilities. Teachers have a more difficult time recognizing learning disabilities when students change schools frequently. When your family moves frequently, it becomes hard for the school system to keep a consistent program in place for you.

Many adults who are dyslexic went through most of their lives without understanding their problem. They knew that they had trouble reading and/or writing, but did not know why. They may have labeled themselves stupid and given up on school by dropping out.

You are more fortunate than they were. Today, schools are better equipped to help students with special needs. Laws have been passed to force schools to provide the services you will need to reach your full potential. Do not be afraid to speak up. Do not give up on school. Instead, become a self-advocate and demand that your school work with you to overcome your disability.

Learning the Truth

The happiest day of my life occurred when I found out that I was dyslexic. I believe that life is about finding solutions and the worst feeling to me is confusion.

Ennis William Cosby

How did you feel when you found out you were dyslexic? Some students feel very depressed. Before a diagnosis, it is possible to believe that learning difficulties will go away—that they can be cured. Once dyslexia is diagnosed, you will realize that your differences will not go away. You will need to work to overcome them. You will need extra time to perform tasks that other students find easy. You will be different.

Other students are relieved. A diagnosis of dyslexia gives a name to your difference. Now you know why you have trouble reading. You know you are not stupid. You know that millions of other people have the same differences. You can begin to use your strengths to overcome your weaknesses. Yes, you know you are different, but now you know how and why. You can begin to deal with it.

How Did Your Parents Feel?

Your parents' reaction to your dyslexia can make a big difference in your life. Your parents can be your advocates and your biggest support. But if they ignore or are embarrassed by your dyslexia, their feelings will add another obstacle for you to overcome.

If your parents continue to deny your difficulties even after your dyslexia has been diagnosed, your life may be harder. Your parents may react with "There is nothing wrong with my kid." They may feel depressed. They may blame the school system for failing to teach you. Some parents may blame themselves. They may decide that since you are dyslexic, you will not be able to go to college or get a job. By lowering their expectations, they may cause you to expect less of yourself. Other parents are glad to finally have a direction. They understand that you will have learning difficulties, and they are ready to do all that they can to help you.

Your parents can be your best advocates, especially if your school is not very sympathetic to the needs of special students. Ask your parents to help you find out as much information as possible. They can read brochures and books and talk to you about them. They can attend conferences and meet with psychologists and counselors. You can learn about dyslexia together.

Your family can also help relieve your social stress. Your school environment may be difficult, but when you get home, you should feel safe and loved. No more pressure to be someone you are not. No more judgments of "stupid" or "slow." Your parents will know how smart and creative you really are.

Behavior Problems

Kids with dyslexia react differently to the social strains that their differences can cause. Some work hard, meeting with teachers and counselors regularly. Others react negatively, making up for lack of self-esteem by creating problems for themselves and those around them.

> *All it is when you perform and people clap for you—it's that these people out there love you for that moment.*
>
> Cher, actress, singer and dyslexic

You may try to distract your teachers and classmates by cracking jokes and entertaining them. While they are laughing and enjoying the show, you feel as if everyone is your friend. They cannot laugh at you if they are laughing with you. You may be able to trick teachers and class-mates into helping you or telling you the answers without their realizing it. As long as they see you smiling, they will not see your pain. You would rather be the class clown than the kid who cannot read.

> *When Billy began school, everyone told him that in first grade he would learn to read. His classmates had learned to read. It seemed easy and fun for them. But Billy just could not catch on. The letters seemed to jump around the page. He was afraid the teacher and his friends would think that he was stupid if they found out. He had to do something.*

By third grade, Billy had developed a way to trick his teachers and classmates into thinking he could read. He even got them to help him.

One day, the kids in his class were taking turns reading out loud. Each student read one sentence. By this time, Billy had memorized a few words that he saw often, like the and is. He had to guess at other words. He listened very carefully to the other kids while they read. He remembered the names of all the characters in the story. When it was his turn to read, he tried to imagine what would happen next.

"Okay, Billy. It is your turn," said Mr. Moffat, his teacher. Billy looked at this sentence: "Mike rode his bike up the street."

Billy smiled at Mr. Moffat. "I'm not sure where to start," he said.

"On page two. The sentence starts 'Mike rode'," said Mr. Moffat.

Billy remembered that in the story, Mike had been looking for his dog by riding his bike around his neighborhood. "Mike rode his bike," said Billy.

"Good. Go on, please" said Mr. Moffat.

Billy looked at the next word. He didn't recognize it. He guessed that Mike was riding to something, so he said "to." He held up two fingers and waved them over his head.

The class laughed. Juan, the boy sitting in the desk next to Billy, called out, "not 'to' . . . 'up'!"

Now Billy was a bit confused. How could a bike be ridden "up"? But he kept laughing. He hopped up and down in his seat. "Up, up, up," he said. The class laughed.

Billy looked at the next word, the, a word he had memorized. Mike rode his bike up the . . . ? What comes next? he thought. Sidewalk seemed as if it had more letters than the word in his sentence. "Street," he guessed out loud.

"Very good, Billy," said Mr. Moffat.

Billy smiled back. He punched his fist into the air over his head. "Yeah!" he cried.

The whole class laughed again. Mr. Moffat chuckled. "Settle down, boys and girls," he said. "Please continue, Amanda."

As Amanda read the next sentence, Billy sighed in relief. He counted how many sentences were left in the story. Only twelve. He counted around the room. He was lucky. The story would be finished before he had another turn. He was safe for one more day.

The longer you cover up your dyslexia, the longer it will be before you get real help. You will not be able to fool your way through life forever.

Some students with learning disabilities withdraw and stay to themselves. They do not talk to their parents. They do not try to make friends with other kids. They are very lonely and afraid.

You may think that the way to avoid rejection is to hide. Maybe you believe that if you do not talk to other kids, they will not find out how stupid you are. Or if they think you are stupid, at least you will not hear them talking about it. Maybe you think that if you sit in the back of the classroom, your teacher will forget that you are there. You may keep your eyes down so he or she will not call on you.

As the bell rang, David took his seat at the last desk in the third row of his classroom. He put his books under his desk and slouched in his chair. He folded his arms across his chest. When his social studies teacher, Mr. Somers, began speaking to the class, David did not look up.

"Please turn to page 142, the Italian Renaissance," said Mr. Somers. "Who can tell me the name of the artist you read about last night?"

Kate raised her hand. "Yes, Kate," said Mr. Somers.

"Michelangelo," Kate answered.

"Right. Who can name some of his statues?"

"The Pieta," called out Seth.

"Good," said Mr. Somers. "Can you name another one . . . David?"

David did not look up. He slouched further in his seat, as if he were trying to disappear under his desk.

"I'll give you a hint," said Mr. Somers. "One of the statues has a name that is very familiar to you."

David shrugged his shoulders. Mr. Somers sighed. "Okay, who can give us the answer?"

"David," called out Kate. "The statue's name is David, too."

I cannot believe how stupid I am, thought David. He scowled. Maybe Mr. Somers had been trying to help me with the answer. But why would anyone try to help me? David thought. Mr. Somers was probably trying to trick me. I hate this class. I know I am going to fail no matter what I do.

Withdrawing will not help and can lead to greater problems. Studies by the U.S. Department of Education have

33

shown that students with learning disabilities are nearly twice as likely to drop out of high school as students without learning disabilities.

Do not hide in the back of the classroom. Speak up for yourself. You are not stupid. You can learn; you just need a different kind of teaching. Your parents or a counselor can help you. By developing a "tough" attitude, you may be able to force other kids to do some of your work for you. Your teachers may need to spend so much time controlling your behavior that they will not discover your real problems. You will end up spending lots of time in detention. In an overcrowded classroom, you may be labeled a troublemaker. Teachers may consider it a waste to spend extra time with a student whose best skill seems to be disrupting the class.

Being the class clown had worked for Anthony for a while. But as his schoolwork got harder, he was less able to cover up. In sixth grade, his teachers thought he was lazy. None of his previous teachers had told his current ones that Anthony could not read.

Eventually, teachers began to call him a smart aleck. They no longer thought that he was cute or funny. When he tried to joke with the class, his teachers called him disruptive. It got worse in junior high. He spent a lot of time in detention.

The other kids started to make fun of him. They stopped laughing with him and started laughing at him.

In high school, Anthony's troubles got worse. One day, Jake followed him out of English. "Boy, are you stupid," said Jake. "Can you even read?"

Anthony turned around and slammed Jake against the lockers. "You better stay away from me, or you'll be sorry."

A teacher came into the hall and caught Anthony. He was suspended for two days. The principal called Anthony's parents, but they talked about his discipline problems, not his learning difficulties.

Anthony had been hiding his reading problems from his parents, too. They could not understand why he kept getting into trouble. Anthony blamed himself for disappointing them.

At school, Anthony's problems got worse. He kept getting into fights. He kept failing his classes.

When he was a junior, Anthony decided there was no point in going to school. He left his house in the morning, like always. But he did not go to his classes. Instead, he spent the day at a video arcade.

Maybe you think that being the troublemaker is better than being the kid with dyslexia. But if you continue on this path, you may earn yourself a new label. Research has shown that 30 percent of adolescents with learning disabilities will be arrested three to five years after dropping out of high school. You may be the high-school dropout. You may be the kid on probation. Or you may be the kid in jail.

Tips for Parents

My parents never made me feel stupid. To them it was important that I knew something about a subject, could apply the knowledge, and could discuss it intelligently.
Paul Orfalea, dyslexic and president of Kinko's

Most of this book is addressed to you, the dyslexic student. This section speaks directly to your parents to help them help you.

Your child is dyslexic. What should you do? First of all, try not to blame yourself. Then search out as much information as possible. The Where to Go for Help section of this book lists organizations that can provide excellent resources. Talk to your child's teacher and your school's guidance counselor. But do not assume that they know everything about what is best for your child.

Remember that your most important job is to advocate for your child. You are his or her primary support and protection. In partnership with your child, you must plan and monitor his or her progress. Do not become an ally with teachers or counselors against your child.

Your child will need your direct help and support when doing homework. You may want to keep a homework log to record the length of time needed to finish assignments. Share this information with your child's teachers. The teacher plans assignments based on how much time most students will need to complete them. The teacher needs to be aware of how much time it takes your child to finish. Sometimes, an assignment will take so long that the stress load may become too great. You may choose to put the assignment aside for a while and come back to it later. However, you may need to make the decision to shorten an assignment. If you find that necessary, write a note to the teacher explaining your decision. Try to end a homework session when your child is having success rather than waiting until he or she has been pushed to exhaustion.

Consider keeping an extra set of textbooks and workbooks at home. Ask the school to supply them. You may want to photocopy extra copies of workbook pages. Recording for the Blind and Dyslexic will record textbooks, but you need to supply them with copies of the books. You also need to give them several weeks' notice. Find out as soon as possible what textbooks your child will need. Your school should be able to tell you by May or June at the latest what books will be needed for the following year.

Find out as much information about dyslexia as possible by attending conferences, reading books, and talking with other parents. Educating yourself will also help you when you are dealing with professionals like educators and counselors. You will also build confidence in your ability to make the right decisions concerning the education and future of your child.

In the summer 1997 issue of *Perspectives*, a publication of the International Dyslexia Association, Cindy Haines suggests creating a notebook of your child's work. "Compile your child's work—everything from crinkled homework sheets, to returned tests, to workbook pages. Organize the papers chronologically and by subject matter. Include anecdotal information as well; these snippets of everyday life may provide you with insights into their language competencies, social relations, and emotional status." This notebook can help you spot trends in your child's learning. You can also use it as evidence of his or her progress or to point out special needs.

Expect the most from your child. This does not mean that you should put extra pressure on him or her. But teachers may lower expectations and make excuses for students with dyslexia. At the same time, maintain a close relationship with your child's teacher. Make it clear that you expect to work in partnership.

Haines also suggests keeping a "master file" of potential references. Tutors, doctors, teachers, psychologists, or counselors may be able to provide insight into the best way to handle your child's disability. "A counselor who deals specifically with college placement for children with learning difficulties may be a useful resource," says Haines. "Although your child may currently be in the sixth grade, you want to prepare for his or her future by securing such a person in case their services are needed."

Talk to your child often about his or her learning difficulty. Keep it from being something scary and bad by honestly discussing how your child learns and why learning seems so hard at times. Be an outlet for frustrations, disappointments, and pain.

Do not forget to praise your child's efforts. Make sure to spend time with your child doing something that you both like to do, just for fun.

Learning Strategies

Nicole felt like the most disorganized person in the world. Her locker was a mess. Every time she opened the door, papers spilled out and sailed to the floor. She only had five minutes between classes, just enough time to grab the papers and jam them back in.

Nicole was always losing her homework. She never had a pen when she needed one. She often found herself in math class with her science book. She had no idea where she had put her copy of Tom Sawyer, the book her English class was reading.

Her lack of organization kept Nicole in a constant state of stress. Her teachers said she was sloppy and irresponsible. Nicole believed them, although she knew she did not mix things up on purpose.

Nicole mixed up time, too, not just things. She never seemed to remember when her assignments were due. She started on one project, then jumped to another. Somehow, nothing seemed to get done.

Nicole needed help.

Learn Self-Discipline

As a dyslexic student, you should realize that you must take control of your learning. Your parents and teachers can help, but you should make the decision to discipline your-self. Take steps to make yourself a successful learner. Some of these tips are simple. Others require more planning.

1. In your classrooms, sit in the front near your teach-ers. It will be easier to pay close attention when you are under your teacher's watchful eye. Try not to sit near the window. Distractions from outside may seem more interesting than your lessons. You want to keep your mind on your work.

2. NEVER skip classes.

3. When ink is required for writing in the classroom, use an erasable pen. Your papers will look neater without a lot of scratching out.

4. Use an expanding file folder instead of many loose folders to keep your schoolwork organized. When you use one folder and keep it with you all the time, you will not need to worry about forget-ting your work.

5. Store extra supplies of pens, pencils, and paper at school. Keep your locker or desk neat and organized.

6. Use technology whenever you are allowed to. Bring a small tape recorder to school to record your teacher's lectures. Tape your ideas or ques-tions so that you can refer to them later. Use a handheld spell checker when you need to write in the classroom. A small electronic diary will help

you remember important assignments and appointments.

7. Keep a list of words that are commonly mixed up, like *there/their*. The list should tell you how and when the words are used.

8. Adhesive notes can be wonderful tools. Use them when you are reading to take notes, to record your ideas or questions, or to organize sections. You may not be allowed to write in your book, but you can stick notes next to the sentences that confuse you.

9. Do not add to your pressure by waiting until the last minute to start working on an assignment. Give yourself plenty of time. It is tempting to avoid an assignment that you do not want to do, especially if you are afraid that it will be hard. If you find yourself thinking, "I can do that project tomorrow," start on it right away!

10. Learn to ask questions without feeling stupid. Many students, not only those with dyslexia, don't ask questions when they don't understand. They think everyone else "gets it." Chances are, you are not the only student who needs more information. By asking questions, you may actually be helping your friends understand, too.

11. Try not to put too much pressure on yourself. This may be difficult to do. You know that to be successful you must work hard. But leave time for something you love to do just for fun.

Watch a movie. Play basketball or go for a hike. You will give your brain some time off to rest and recover.

Take Your Brain to Camp

One way to give your brain a rest is to send it to camp. Summer camp can offer a great opportunity to spend a week or two getting away from it all. You can try a new activity or sport. You will have a chance to make new friends who understand your dyslexia. These friendships can last a lifetime.

Before going to camp, you will need to make some decisions about the kind of camp you prefer. Then collect information about camps that offer that kind of experience.

Your first decision should be whether you want to go to a residential (or "sleep-over") camp or a day camp. You will have more questions and different considerations if you decide to spend a week or two away from home.

Like day camps, residential camps provide sports and recreational activities. But because you will be living on your own, they also promote independence. You will live under the supervision of a trained staff. But the members of this staff will expect you to take care of yourself. Be sure that you will be ready to live away from home for the length of the camp program. You may want to choose a short overnight stay for your first experience.

You should also decide if you would like to go to a special camp for kids with learning disabilities or a camp with a different focus, like a sports camp. Some camps are set up to include campers with and without disabilities. Some camps for disabled kids include campers with all kinds of disabilities, physical, emotional, and learning. Others specialize in a particular type of disability.

Finally, some camps are strictly recreational. Others offer instructional and remedial programs. You should decide if you want your camp experience to include learning. Or do you just want to let loose and have fun?

After you have narrowed your choice to a specific kind of camp, you will need to think about other needs.

1.   Some camps are coed. Others are only for boys or girls. Do you want to deal with the social demands of a coed camp?

2.   Some camps have hundreds of campers per session. Others have less than fifty. Will you feel comfortable among throngs of kids? Or will you feel lost?

3.   If you choose a camp that is part instructional and part recreational, find out the daily schedule. How much time will be spent on each activity?

4.   What kind of location are you looking for? You can choose a camp with cabins around a lake. Some camps are held at schools or colleges that do not hold classes during the summer.

5.   If you are choosing a residential camp, check out the living facilities. Will you sleep in bunks or a college dormitory? What are the dining facilities like? What is the typical menu? Where are the bathrooms and showers? Some camps are very rustic—real camping. Others are more luxurious.

6.   Ask about staffing. How many counselors are on staff compared to the number of campers? The American Camping Association recommends one staff member for every four learning disabled campers. Staffing in nonspecial camps, however, can be as high as one counselor for every eight campers.

7.   Find out specific information about the programs offered. How will you choose your activities? Will you register ahead of time and be sure you will be enrolled? Or will you sign up at camp on a first-come-first-served basis?

Finally, to protect yourself, you will want to know the answers to some technical questions. Is the camp insured? What are the health care and emergency procedures? Is there a nurse or other heath professional on staff? How are the counselors trained? Is the camp accredited by the American Camping Association? How does the camp communicate with parents? Will you be allowed to call home? Can your parents reach you by phone?

The best way to find out about a camp is to talk to someone who went there. You may want to ask your friends where they have gone. Or ask the camp to give you the names of some previous campers.

Documenting Your Dyslexia

As a pupil, I was neither particularly good nor bad. My principal weakness was a poor memory, and especially a poor memory for words and texts.

Albert Einstein

Under the Americans with Disabilities Act, people with learning disabilities are guaranteed the right to equal access to programs and services. Once your dyslexia is documented, your school is required by law to provide accommodations and modifications that will help you learn. In order to qualify for these accommodations, you must be certified as learning disabled.

The documentation of your dyslexia must be provided by a qualified professional. This person, usually a psychologist or medical doctor, should have direct experience working with adolescents who are learning disabled. The purpose of your assessment will be to show that dyslexia greatly limits your ability to learn under standard teaching methods. The assessment will make specific recommendations for accommodations to help you learn. It will also explain why these accommodations are necessary.

You will need to have an interview with a psychologist. When talking with him or her, you should be as honest and frank as possible. The psychologist will not be able to provide an accurate assessment if you attempt to cover up or exaggerate your dyslexia. You need to show how your dyslexia affects your schoolwork or your ability to learn. You should give the psychologist as much information as possible, including copies of school grade reports or test scores.

The psychologist may also want to speak with other members of your family. He or she will probably request copies of your medical records. You will probably also be asked to take tests that the psychologist chooses.

The International Dyslexia Association recommends that these tests and information be included in an assessment for dyslexia:

1. A developmental, medical, behavioral, academic, and family history.

2. Information on your ability to process language.

3. Information on your ability to understand what you hear and read.

4. Information on your ability to coordinate your motor skills with your eyes.

5. Information on your memory and ability to reason.

6. Specific language tests to show your ability to understand how words and letters relate to sound.

7. Educational tests to show the level of your basic skills in reading, math, written language, and

spelling. This testing should include oral and silent reading, reading comprehension, handwriting, sentence and paragraph writing, and dictated spelling.

8.   A classroom observation.

You will need to work closely with the professional who conducts your assessment. The Association on Higher Education and Disability (AHEAD) provides these recommendations to help students and their parents work with a qualified professional during the assessment process:

1.   Ask the professional what his or her credentials are. What experience has he or she had working with adolescents with learning disabilities, particularly dyslexia? If you are planning to attend college, ask if he or she has ever worked with the office of special services at the school where you will be applying.

2.   Encourage the professional to work with the counselor at your high school and to ask questions if he or she needs additional information.

3.   Be prepared to be honest and frank and to provide any information the professional requests.

4.   After your assessment is complete, ask for a written copy. Ask for the chance to talk with the professional about the results and recommendations.

5.   Keep a personal file of all your records and reports.

Over time, your educational needs and abilities may change. You may need to request a new evaluation that reflects those changes. Remember, you must be ready to speak on your own behalf.

Individual Education Program

Your Individual Education Program (IEP) will be set up based on the results of your assessment and testing. Its purpose is to help you manage your special education program. You will work with your parents, teachers, and counselor to set up tools that will best fit your needs.

The IEP is a written document. The school agrees to provide the assistive technology, special services, or tutoring as recommended by your evaluation. By agreeing to your IEP, your school makes a commitment to your education.

Your IEP will be developed during a meeting with teachers, counselors, and your parents. The International Dyslexia Association recommends that you talk over some ideas with your parents before the meeting:

1. Make a list of your strengths and weaknesses. What do you do well? What concerns do you have about reading, writing, math, behavior, organization, and communication? How can you develop self-advocacy skills?

2. List your goals for the future. What are your plans after you graduate from high school?

3. Understand your goals for the next year. Which

49

goal is most important? What will you need to do to meet your goals? How can the school help you?

4.   Ask your school guidance counselor for a copy of a draft IEP.

During the IEP meeting, you will work with your counselor, parents, and teachers to develop annual goals. These goals should say what you can reasonably be expected to do in a year. Be sure that you understand specifically what these goals are. General goals, like "improve writing skills," will be difficult to assess. How will you improve your writing skills? What will you need to do?

You will also discuss any accommodations that you need, including special services and equipment. Work with your school to determine if assistive technology will be provided. Perhaps you will be allowed to use special equipment, but will be responsible for supplying it. The IEP should be very specific about what services will be provided. How many hours a week will you receive special services? On what day will services begin? When will they end?

Finalizing your IEP may take more than one meeting. Also, at any time you can ask that your IEP be reviewed and reevaluated. At the very least, your IEP should be reviewed every year.

Assistive Technology

You probably don't have your own secretary. So, you may need assistive technology, like a computer with a word-processing program. Assistive technology is a piece of equipment or a computer program that will help you work around, or compensate, for your dyslexia. Tape recorders, calculators, spell checkers, and computers can all be used to assist you.

At this time, early in the twenty-first century, researchers do not have a cure for dyslexia. You must learn to live with it. However, assistive technology can relieve some of the pressure that learning causes. These devices can help you communicate with others. They can help you organize your ideas, your studies, and your time. Educators recommend, however, that you use assistive technology as part of a general learning program. Use it as one of your learning tools.

Do not rely on assistive technology to do everything for you. Equipment can break down. Batteries wear out at critical times. For example, take written notes (or make arrangements to borrow another student's notes) at the same time that you record a lecture. If the tape breaks or the batteries die, you will not be at a total loss.

Assistive computer software is not the same as instructional software. The purpose of instructional software is to improve your writing or reading skills. Assistive technology will not improve your skills. It helps you work around your dyslexia. For example, a spell checker points out words that are spelled incorrectly so that you can change them. It does not explain spelling rules or provide practice exercises that can improve your spelling.

Many simple and relatively low-cost items can be very helpful. Handheld spell checkers and pocket calculators can be carried to the library, the grocery store, or a friend's house. Tape recorders can be used to record instructions at school or on the job. They can also play books on tape to help with reading assignments. Larger, more complex, and less portable equipment is also available. Reading machines read books out loud using a computerized voice. Voice-recognition software lets you enter information by talking to a computer. You can "write" stories by telling them to the computer. Talking calculators can read back numbers as you work, helping you to correct transposed numbers, like 79 for 97.

As you get older, assistive technology can help you live more independently. You will probably need to ask friends and family for help less often. Completing a task successfully on your own will boost your self-esteem and give you more confidence.

Kinds of Assistive Technology

Four general groups of assistive technology can help you work around your dyslexia: reading assistance, writing assistance, listening assistance, and assistance in organizing time and information. Dyslexia affects each person differently. Only you can decide which equipment or software will work best for you.

Reading Assistance

Reading machines are computers that "read" text out loud. The technical term for these devices is optical character recognition systems, or OCRs. Some OCRs are part of a personal computer; others stand alone. An OCR lets you input printed text, using a scanner, directly into a computer. The computer translates the printed text into electronic signals that the computer understands. A computer, or synthesized voice, "speaks" the text out loud. It may be easier for you to understand what you hear than it is to understand what you read. If this is true, you may find an OCR system helpful.

You may also be able to use texts that have been recorded on computer discs or CD-ROMs. These do not require an OCR system because the text does not need to be scanned into the computer. Most personal computers with a CD-ROM drive will be able to use these discs. Recording for the Blind and Dyslexic has begun recording texts on computer discs in addition to audiotapes. These texts are called "books on disc." Tape recorders are the most common and least expensive form of reading assistance. Books on tape are widely available in bookstores, on-line, and in public libraries.

Writing Assistance

I like the written language because I like photo-copying. I believe in double spacing, since it helps my business.

Paul Orfalea

Word-processing programs help many people, not just those with dyslexia, write more clearly and with less effort. First, they eliminate the need for constructing individual letters with a pen. As your typing skills improve with practice, words flow freely and with little effort. Word-processing programs are equipped with tools to correct spelling. Many are now able to interpret sentences and change some spelling automatically. The newest programs include word prediction. The program will guess the word it "thinks" that you are typing and show you the word. Word processors let you change or delete words without smudging your paper with erasures. They also let you move sentences and paragraphs without recopying your paper. It will be typed on your computer's printer in clean type that is easy to read and looks professional.

Grammar-checking or proofreading programs are also usually part of word-processing programs. When the computer suspects errors in grammar, punctuation, capitalization, or word choice, the sentence is highlighted. The computer offers suggestions for changes. You decide whether the changes should be made. Grammar checkers also spot errors in spelling that may have been overlooked by the spell checker. For example, spelling errors involving words that are spelled the same but sound differently, like *there/their* and *to/too*, will not be highlighted by a spell checker. The word usage error may be uncovered by the grammar checker.

You do need to be careful using a grammar-checking program. The corrections it highlights should be considered, but you should not make the changes automatically. Sometimes, the sentence will be correct the way you originally write it.

Some word processors also include outlining programs. The program automatically creates outlines with Roman numerals for major headings, and numbers and letters for details. As you add or change information, the computer rearranges the headings. You can enter your ideas as they come to you. The outlining program makes reorganizing much easier.

Although not part of most word-processing programs, "bubble" programs, or "web charts," are available to help you organize your ideas. Some students with dyslexia find these programs helpful because they create pictures, or graphic representations, of your ideas and how they connect to each other.

Using a word processor has emotional benefits as well. Writing can be much less stressful. You may have dysgraphia, difficulty constructing letters. The anxiety this causes can be lessened. Errors can be corrected easily. You can let your ideas flow freely without encountering the frustration of your writing difficulties.

Speech recognition systems let you talk to your computer. Rather than typing in commands or text for a paper, you dictate your ideas by using a microphone. Most systems need a slight pause between words. As technology improves, however, you will most likely be able to speak normally and your computer will record your words. If you use a speech recognition system often, the system will get better at recognizing your tone and "understand" your words more easily.

Using a speech synthesizer, like the reading program already discussed, the computer can read your writing back to you. Your dyslexia may cause you to have difficulty reading what you have written. Using this speaking program, you can read your words on the screen at the same time that the computer reads them out loud. Hearing and reading the words at the same time may help you recognize errors. It may also help you make changes in the organization or sentence structure of your work.

To carry this technology with you to school, you would need a laptop computer. Laptops can be expensive. An alternative is a "smart keyboard." Smart keyboards usually run on regular batteries. They don't use a rechargeable battery that could run down in the middle of an assignment. It's easy to carry a supply of batteries, but it may not be so easy to find a place to plug in your laptop. Smart keyboards can be used for spell checking or note taking. You can use them to list homework assignments. You can also begin writing projects that you will finish when you get home. When choosing a smart keyboard, you should select one that is easy to operate. You don't need a fancy, complex machine with functions you will never use.

Listening Assistance

Tape recorders are the most obvious tool of listening assistance. Tape your teacher's lecture. You can play it over as many times as you need to. You can also replay and concentrate on particular sections of the lecture.

Personal listening systems transmit sounds directly from a speaker wearing a small microphone to a listener wearing a headphone. You may have seen one of these headphones in a theater. Many larger theaters offer this system to the hearing impaired. The words spoken by the actors are picked up by the microphone and transmitted directly to the listener's ear. The listener controls the volume. While you may not have a hearing disability, you may have difficulty focusing on spoken words. This can be especially true during a classroom lecture. You may be able to arrange for your teacher or professor to wear a microphone. A voice sent directly into your ear is difficult to ignore.

Assistance in Organization

A personal data manager is a handheld computer that helps you to organize time and information. These managers keep track of personal information like phone numbers, addresses, appointments, and important dates. They can also show reminders. Most managers have a small screen that displays information. You enter information using a keypad.

Personal organizational software is also available for your personal computer. You can use these programs to remind yourself of important events or tasks you need to complete. If your dyslexia makes it difficult for you to organize your time or remember important information, a personal data manager may help you.

Choosing Assistive Technology

Only you can decide what assistive technology will best fit your needs. You need to understand where your weaknesses lie. Technology changes very quickly. Equipment and programs available today may be out of date in a few months. Make it your responsibility to get the most current information.

Keep the cost in mind. Simple and low-cost equipment, like portable tape recorders, can do a lot to make your life easier. The Schwab Foundation for Learning offers this advice to help you choose assistive technology:

1. Identify your strengths. Assistive technology not only compensates for your weaknesses, it also takes advantage of your strengths. While you may have difficulty reading written words, you may easily understand spoken words. Technology that changes written words to speech, like an OCR or speech synthesizer, might help you.

2. Be sure that your parents or counselors include you in the selection process. You are the one who will use the technology. You may be able to experiment with the equipment by arranging a trial or loan period. Go to computer or trade shows where equipment is demonstrated.

3. Choose the technology based on your strengths and weaknesses. There is no point in paying for technology you do not need or cannot use. Just because equipment is the latest thing does not mean it is the best choice.

4. Consider the location. Where and how will you use the technology? Will you use your new computer or tape recorder at school or at work? Where will you put it? Do you need a new desk or storage cabinet? Will you need a voice synthesizer to help you learn technical information or an audiotape of an actor reading *To Kill a Mockingbird*?

5. Consider portability. Will you need to take it with you? A pocket-sized spell checker can go with you to school. Your personal computer cannot.

6. Choose technologies that can work together. Will the voice synthesizer you are considering work with your personal computer? A new computer to run the synthesizer could greatly increase your expense.

7. Choose technologies that you can learn to use. The commands should be simple and easy to perform. Technology that is difficult to use will add to your frustration. Find out if the company that makes your equipment has an on-line help site.

8. Consider the warranty and technical support. Choose equipment from companies that offer toll-free numbers or field representatives in locations near you.

Preparing for College

Yes, college is an option for dyslexic people. But you must be willing to work hard. Most students begin to actively prepare for college in their junior year of high school. But students with dyslexia must begin their journey toward college as freshmen. If you are thinking of college as a possibility, begin to prepare right away to be sure that you have the skills you will need. You will also want to develop a support system that includes your parents, counselors, and teachers.

Once you have made the decision to work toward college, you must be ready to take control of your future. You will probably need help. But one of the most important parts of your preparation will be to teach yourself to be independent. You will need to develop emotional strength and social skills that will help you cope with your new college environment. Once you leave high school, you will be responsible for yourself.

This may seem scary, but in reality it is a destiny faced by all students entering college. Your parents and teachers will help you get there. But once you are there you are on your own. Success comes from preparing for that independence. Preparation will give you the courage and self-confidence to succeed.

Now that you see where you are headed, go back to where you are: in high school. You think you want to go to college. Where should you begin?

You and your parents should set up a transitional planning meeting with your school counselors. Your high school is required by law to help you plan your future after graduation. Begin this process as soon as possible; your freshman year is the best time to start. By starting right away, you will build a foundation of skills that will make the transition to college easier. The fact that these skills will also help you while you are still in high school is an added benefit. You will develop compensatory skills—skills that help you work around, or compensate for, your disability. You will work on study skills and organizational skills, especially the ability to organize your time. You should also begin to learn self-advocacy. Up to now, your parents have probably worked closely with your school on your behalf. You need to learn how to do this for yourself. You also need to look at yourself. What is your learning style and how will that affect your individual needs?

There is a lot to learn. You need to begin on the basics right away. Your junior and senior years will be devoted to the specific search for a college. Right now, you need the skills to get you there.

Freshman Year

During your freshman year, work with your counselor to choose courses in which you will be successful. These courses should also fill the requirements you will need for college admission. You may want to choose electives, like art, that give you some relief from academic pressures. Develop a four-year plan. Throughout high school, at least once a year, you should meet with your counselor to discuss changes to your program that may be needed.

Begin to learn skills to help you compensate for your dyslexia. Most importantly, learn to use a computer. Computers can relieve you of the need to write by hand and can check your spelling and grammar. Some computers recognize voice commands and can produce text directly from dictation. Using a computer effectively is one of the most important skills to learn. Also, be aware of the newest computer technology. Know what equipment and software are available to help you.

Study Skills

Work on your study skills. Most college-bound students can benefit from a course in study skills. Unfortunately, most schools do not offer one. Study skills give students the tools and training they need to succeed in school.

Organize, organize, organize. All students need to keep their notes and assignments organized. They need to be aware of how much time each assignment will take. Assignments take longer for most dyslexic students, so organizing is even more important for you.

Time can be your enemy. The last thing you want to do is waste it. A disorganized pile of notes can be a big time waster. You do not want to search through folders, assignment pads, and notebooks to find the description of your assignment before you can begin.

Some schools include advice about organization in their classroom instruction. Teachers may tell you how to set up your notebook with dividers for different topics. They may show you how to make a weekly homework chart to keep your assignments straight. They may even suggest a way to set up your study space at home. These are all skills you will need. If your teachers do not help you with them, look for a study skills class outside of your school. Or arrange time after school to ask your teacher for help.

Study skills also include techniques for taking notes, summarizing what you read, and understanding the main ideas of what you read. Like any new skill, they will need to be practiced. Note-taking skills include learning how to abbreviate and edit. Skills in summarizing and understanding the main ideas will help you pick out the important information from what you read. These skills are especially important when you are reading something long and complicated, like a college textbook.

Study skills are important for all students. Dyslexia can make organization particularly hard, while at the same time making the need for it greater. Practicing organizational skills will be especially important for you.

Extracurricular Activities

Take time to become involved in extracurricular activities. Give yourself a break from your struggle with schoolwork to do something you enjoy. Many people with dyslexia are especially good in sports or art. Playing on a sports team will boost your self-esteem. If you are artistic, you might choose to work on the scenery for the school play. You will probably make new friends. They will see you as the center on the football team or a great painter rather than the "kid with dyslexia." Also, colleges and universities will be impressed by your abilities. They will be more likely to accept a student who can contribute to the university's athletic or drama program.

Learn About Your Own Dyslexia

Dyslexia is a general term for your learning disability. But dyslexia affects each person differently. Understand how it affects you. Be able to describe your particular strengths and weaknesses. Word your description in as positive and matter-of-fact a way as possible. For example, rather than beginning "I am really bad at . . ." or "It takes me forever to . . ." say "I need to plan ahead to . . ." or "I need to spend extra time on . . ." In addition, describe your particular talents. Include "I am very creative" or "I am a great baseball player" in your description. Practice talking about how dyslexia affects you now. Then you will be more prepared when the time comes for college visits and interviews.

Sophomore Year

Begin each year of high school by meeting with your counselor. Discuss the courses you have chosen. Try to take as many "mainstream" courses as possible. These are courses open to all students. As you direct your education toward your goal to attend college, evaluate which study techniques are working for you. Some will need to be changed to better fit your needs. Keep practicing the skills that work.

It is time to begin to look at colleges and to think about your future career. These two objectives work together. Like all college students, you will want to choose a college that provides the best academic preparation for your chosen career. So it is best to have some idea of what that career will be. You know what interests you. Begin to investigate what careers use those interests. Many resources are available to help you understand what kinds of training and skills are needed for different jobs. They are probably available in your school or town library. Your counselor should also be a resource for career information. Do not put too much pressure on yourself at this stage. You can always change your mind.

Junior Year

This is crunch time. During your junior year, you will evaluate colleges, choose those that interest you most, and begin the application process. Like all college-bound juniors, you will set up college interviews and take the ACT or SAT college preparatory exams.

Senior Year

The final steps of your college application process will occur during the first half of your senior year. You will have narrowed your choices to three to five colleges or universities. You will submit the final applications. You may decide to retake the SAT. Once the applications and all required educational materials have been submitted, you will simply wait. You should be notified of your acceptance in early spring, usually March or April. Hopefully, you will then make a final evaluation among the colleges that have accepted you. You will make your final choice and let that college or university know that you will be part of its new freshman class.

ACT/SAT
Modifications

Most colleges require the ACT (American College Testing) program test or the SAT (Scholastic Assessment Test) as part of the admission process. By law, students who have been documented as dyslexic must be given the option to use special accommodations when taking these tests.

Your dyslexia must have been documented. That means you must have completed an assessment by a qualified professional. Since you are probably receiving special services at your school, this assessment has probably been completed. You may need to provide documentation to the testing agency.

ACT

The ACT is made up of four parts: English, math, reading, and science reasoning. When registering for the ACT, you must complete and return the request for ACT assessment special testing. On this form, you will specify "dyslexia" as your learning disability. You must also state that an IEP is on file at your school. Your IEP should show that the accommodations you are requesting are necessary. Special testing conditions include extended time, large print test booklets, audiocassette versions, or the use of a reader.

The standard ACT tests are given on national dates and at locations that have been prescheduled. Testing for special needs, however, will be arranged at a time that is convenient for you and the person who will supervise, usually a teacher or guidance counselor. You will probably take the test at your school.

SAT

The SAT has two sections: verbal and math. To request special testing accommodations, you will need to fill out two forms: the SAT registration form and the eligibility form for students with disabilities. To qualify for special testing, you must meet these four criteria: "(a) have a disability that necessitates testing accommodations; (b) have documentation on file at school that supports the need for accommodations; (c) receive special accommodations for school-based tests; and (d) complete an eligibility form."

It is possible to receive special testing for the SAT if you do not receive special services at school. In that case, documentation must be presented to the SAT board for review. Special testing accommodations for SATs include extended time, large type, an audiocassette with regular or large type, a reader's script with regular or large type, and large-block answer sheets. If you use these accommodations, you may take the test within a twelve-day period of a regularly scheduled standard test. Most likely, the test will be given at your school.

The College Search

What exactly are the steps necessary for evaluating a college or university? How is college different from high school? What questions should you ask? What questions can you expect to be asked? Preparation for this process can help relieve your stress and anxiety.

College is different from high school in many ways. Most of these differences reflect the expectation that students will take responsibility for themselves and their learning. College students receive much less individual attention. They are not usually forced to go to class. The short-term homework assignments designed to determine whether students are keeping up with reading may not exist. Exams are few and test large amounts of material. Extra-credit work is not usually offered. Professors don't always review information before an exam. They are also unlikely to distribute outlines or study guides.

This learning independence will be a new kind of freedom. Your parents and teachers will not be looking over your shoulder to be sure that you have finished your work or studied for your exam. But many new college students, dyslexic or not, use this freedom to spend more time on socializing and less on their studies. The result can be disastrous. To avoid this trap, you will need to practice self-discipline. Without it, you can quickly fall behind.

College Selection

I had difficulty reading. Math was and still is almost impossible for me. My brain scrambles images that my eyes see. But once I got the hang of it, I went on in school. I even ended up graduating from college, and getting my Ph.D. in art history.

Patricia Polacco, *Firetalking*

Choosing a college or university is a difficult decision for any student. It involves a great deal of preparation and investigation. In addition to the academic issues that concern all students, those with dyslexia also need to determine what special services are offered by the school.

Before you begin looking at colleges, you need to look at yourself. Determine what your particular needs and interests are. What are your future goals? In what kind of social environment do you feel most comfortable? How far from home are you willing to travel? Do you plan to commute from home or live at school? Answering these questions will narrow your search.

Which colleges or universities offer the academic programs that interest you? Like any student preparing for college, you may not yet be certain what your major will be. If you are unsure about your college major, you may want to enroll in a two-year community college at first. You may feel less pressured in this environment.

Choosing a College or University

If you are not good at reading, do something else. Go where you are strong.

Paul Orfalea

Most high school students begin their search for a college by discussing their needs with their counselor. Your counselor will probably have recommendations based on what he or she believes are your academic strengths and weaknesses. These recommendations will also be based on your interests. But do not limit yourself to the choices made by your counselor. Only you really know what is important to you.

Many colleges send admission representatives to high schools. These representatives meet with groups of students who may be interested in attending their schools. By going to these meetings, you will have a chance to ask general questions in a less stressful environment than an individual interview. Although you probably will not ask questions specifically relating to your dyslexia at these presentations, you can find out about academic programs, athletic programs, and general support services, like writing labs and computer labs. You can also ask general questions about the school, like the number of students attending, and the

71

number of students who live on campus or commute. What are the dormitories like? How close is the campus to a town? Asking in person rather than relying on printed brochures and catalogs may give you a better feel for the university.

Many college reference guides are available to help you. You can probably find one of these guides in your school or public library. You may also find copies in your counselor's office. Paperback versions are available in most bookstores. Some include CD-ROMs. The guides include profiles of hundreds of colleges and universities. They are very good resources to help you begin your search. After looking through these guides, you can request additional information from the colleges or universities that seem to best fit your needs.

In addition to the general questions asked by all high school students preparing for college, you will have additional concerns. You need to choose a school that offers you the best opportunity for success by providing the services you need to work with your dyslexia. How sensitive is the college or university to the needs of students with learning disabilities?

When Anita Bell and her parents, Sarah and Bob, drove through the gates of Woodbridge College, they fell in love with the campus. Tall oak trees lined the driveway. Brick buildings that looked like mansions instead of class buildings stood behind large lawns crisscrossed by stone paths. "This is perfect," said Anita. "It's just the way I imagined college would be."
"It is beautiful, but do not make up your mind yet,"

said Sarah. "Remember the phrase 'Don't judge a book by its cover.' You cannot decide which college you want just on the way it looks."

"Okay," said Anita. "But so far, it looks great!"

"We can park the car and walk around," said Bob. "We have about fifteen minutes before our appointment with the admissions office."

They parked behind the admissions building and walked around to the front. It was one of four buildings facing a large area of grass and trees. The other buildings included the student center/dining hall and two dormitories. Students sat on the ground or on benches reading and talking. Some boys were tossing a football.

"Looks like nobody goes to class," said Bob.

"Come on, Dad," said Anita. "You know they probably only have two or three classes today. It is a beautiful day. Of course everyone wants to be outside."

Anita and her parents followed the path past the student center to the library. Inside, they saw that the library used a computerized cataloging system for books and periodicals. "That will make it easier for me to find what I need," said Anita.

They walked back to the admissions office to meet with a counselor.

"Remember, honey, this is just a preliminary meeting," said Bob. "Do not be nervous. We want to find out what services Woodbridge has to offer. We also need to ask about their art department. In fact, they are the ones who should be nervous. They will be trying to sell themselves to us."

"Somehow, I doubt that they are nervous," said Anita.

The Bells were met in the lobby by a young blond woman. "Hi, I am Maggie Magill," she said.

Anita held out her hand. "I'm Anita Bell," she said. She shook Ms. Magill's hand firmly, looking her straight in the eye. "I am here to find out about Woodbridge College."

"Great," said Ms. Magill. "You can all come into my office and sit down. Anita, you take the chair in front of my desk, please.

"What brings you to Woodbridge College, Anita?" asked Ms. Magill.

"My school guidance counselor suggested Woodbridge because you have a very good art department," answered Anita.

"What kind of art are you interested in?" asked Ms. Magill.

"I am a sculptor, and I am interested in ceramics. I understand that you have a pottery studio here."

"That's right," said Ms. Magill. "After we finish talking, one of our students, Becky Chase, will take you on a tour of the campus. She will take you to the art building. She is also an art major. You can ask her any questions you may have about the program.

"I can tell you that our art department is very strong. Our faculty members are working artists as well as professors. The classes are small, so you will get plenty of individual attention. We also keep the studios open until 10:00 every night and all day on the weekends, so students can work on their projects independently. We encourage students to try different types of art, something they may not have done before."

"I would like to try photography," said Anita. "Do you have a darkroom?"

"Yes, we do," said Ms. Magill.

A tall, dark-haired student stuck her head in the door of Ms. Magill's office.

"Hi, Ms. Magill," she said.

"Hi, Becky," said Ms Magill. "This is Anita Bell and her parents, Sarah and Bob. Anita wants to be an art major, too."

"Great, I will show her around." Becky tuned to Anita. "I love it here," she said. "The professors are wonderful. Not too pushy or critical. Very supportive. My drawing professor took us all to a gallery opening last weekend. It was awesome!

"Come on. I can show you my dorm room, the student center, the gym, and the library. We can walk through the classroom buildings. The food here is okay—not great, but okay. Fortunately, there is a pizza place that delivers on campus."

"I'll talk to you some more when you come back," said Ms. Magill.

After you have narrowed your search to a few colleges or universities, talk to the admissions staff. Ask careful specific questions. You may choose to talk frankly about your dyslexia. Emphasize your strengths but recognize that you will need help. Demonstrating that you understand how to succeed with your dyslexia by talking openly and confidently about it may put college representatives more at ease.

Find out if the admissions procedures are different for students with dyslexia. There may be a special application or testing. Recommendations may be required from your high school counselor or other educator.

Find out the special services offered by the school. Is there an office of support services? Does the college offer remedial or developmental courses? Can the curriculum be changed, for example, to waive the foreign language requirement? How many students are served by support services? What percentage of them graduate? Are there additional fees for these services? You, your parents, and your counselor should prepare specific questions that relate to your needs. There are over ninety colleges with comprehensive special services programs in the United States. Find out as much information as possible to make the most educated selection. You may find that no one college or university offers everything you need or want. Look for the program that offers the greatest chance of success with the least amount of stress.

Anita and her parents returned with Becky to Ms. Magill's office.

"Thanks for your help, Becky," said Ms.Magill.

"No problem," said Becky. She handed Anita a piece of paper. "Here is my phone number and e-mail address. If you have any more questions, let me know."

"Thanks," said Anita.

After Becky left, the Bells sat down in Ms. Magill's office again.

"We really liked the campus," said Sarah. "The art studios are great. But we have some other questions. As you know, Anita is dyslexic. We need to talk specifically about how she will fit in here and how her dyslexia will be handled."

"I am aware of this," said Ms. Magill. "I have asked Mr. Bush, our director of support services, to meet with you. He should be here any minute. In the meantime, let me tell you that we have services available to all students. Our writing lab connects students who need help writing essays with students who are good writers. The students working in the writing lab can help Anita to organize her research and edit drafts of her papers. We have two computer labs, one in the student center and one in the science building. They are open from 7:00 AM until midnight every day. These labs are available to everyone, not just students with special needs."

A short, balding man walked into Ms. Magill's office.

"This is Anita Bell and her parents, Sarah and Bob," said Ms. Magill. "This is Mr. Bush, the director of our office of support services."

"I am here to answer your questions about the services we offer students with special needs," said Mr. Bush. "What accommodations do you think you might need, Anita?"

"You know that I am dyslexic," said Anita. "So I have trouble reading and writing. Basically, it takes me a longer time to read through something. If I have to rush, it is a big waste because I will not remember anything I read. I need to take my time and read carefully. My handwriting is pretty bad, so if I have to write in class, my work can be really hard for the teacher to understand. I have a spell checker, but I still make spelling mistakes. I do a lot better when I can take the writing assignment home and work on it *on my computer. It would be easier for the teacher to read, too."*

"We can usually make arrangements with professors to allow students with special needs to take their writing assignments home. What about tests?"

"If it is an essay test, again, I would like to work on it on my computer. If it is a multiple-choice or true/false test, with a lot of questions, it helps if someone reads it to me. In high school, I had a teacher who read the test into a tape recorder. I played the test tape in my cassette player with headphones, so I did not disturb the other students. The tape worked well because I could rewind it and play the questions again if I needed to."

"That kind of accommodation will need to be worked out with your professors," said Mr. Bush. "Some professors are more cooperative than others. Yes, they are required to make accommodations. But if they really do not want to, they sometimes take it out on the student. I know which professors are the most difficult to deal with, so when you are making your course selections, let me give you a hand. I can steer you away from a difficult situation."

"Basically, my office is set up to help you be successful here at Woodbridge," said Mr. Bush. "We have a very active support group that meets once a week just to talk. A lot of kids get frustrated or feel stressed out. Talking to other kids who understand can be a big help. We also have groups of kids that meet to study together. We mix kids who do not have special needs with those who do. We find working together helps. You will also make new friends that way. We have tutors available, too.

"One thing we stress, though, is self-discipline. You will not find much sympathy if you have been goofing off and spending too much time partying. We are here to help you, but we expect you to help yourself. You will need to spend more time studying than other students do. That may not seem fair, but it is true. If you are not willing to make the commitment, you probably should not come to Woodbridge."

"Thanks for being so honest," said Anita. "I have a lot to think about. I love this campus. I know college can be scary, but I think I am ready."

Of course, the college admissions representative will also have questions for you. It is very important to be able to talk about your dyslexia confidently. You know it will not go away, and you know how to deal with it successfully. You understand your strengths and weaknesses. The university may want to know what accommodations you will need. Tell them what you use in high school. Be ready to talk about why you have chosen your course of study and career goals. Why do you believe you will be successful? Why is your choice realistic? Be prepared to discuss how your high school work has prepared you for college. Have you taken college prep courses?

On the drive home, Anita and her parents talked about their day at Woodbridge College.

"What did you think, honey?" Sarah asked Anita.

"The art program is great," Anita said. "I do not think I would have a problem there. I am not sure about the academic requirements. I need to look at

them again. I forgot to ask Mr. Bush if they will waive the foreign language requirement. Maybe I can take a different course instead. I think I need to talk to Ms. Osborne when I get back to school and see how she thinks I would do at Woodbridge."

"That is a good idea," said Bob. "She has been your counselor all through high school. I am sure she will have some suggestions. Maybe she knows where you can take a study skills course."

"I really like Woodbridge," said Anita. "I felt comfortable on campus. The other kids seemed to be really nice. I want to try and work it out."

"We will do our best to help you, honey," said Sarah.

It will be very important to convince the admissions representative that you can advocate for yourself. Show that you understand that college is different from high school and that you are prepared to take responsibility for dyslexia and to find the support you need.

Preparing for a College Admissions Interview

College admissions interviews are stressful for all students. You want to make a favorable impression. Speak as clearly and confidently as possible. That does not mean you should blurt out the first thing that comes into your mind. There is no disadvantage in taking a few moments to think about your answer. When you do answer, look directly at the interviewer and speak with authority.

You will feel more confident if you have prepared for the interview ahead of time. The published guidebooks to colleges and universities include questions that most students can expect to be asked. The interviewer may ask these questions: Which high school courses were the easiest or hardest? Which high school courses were your favorite or least favorite? What are your long-term goals? You should also be prepared to talk about your high school: the size of the student body, the academic competitiveness, the percentage of students who go on to college, extracurricular activities. You may also be asked questions that seem to have nothing to do with your application. For example, you may be asked to talk about how you spent your summer, a favorite trip you took with your family, or a book you have read recently.

Prepare answers to these questions and practice interviewing with someone, like your parents. Practicing in a less stressful environment will help you feel more confident during the real interview. There is no reason why you should not bring notes to the interview. You may want to write them on 3 x 5 index cards. Write notes to remind you of your questions. You can also write down some facts you want to be sure to mention about yourself.

You may want to bring a tape recorder and ask to record the interview. This will help you to remember the important information you receive. Taping the interview may also relieve you of the stress of attempting to remember everything you hear while preparing to answer the next question.

At the end of the interview, ask the interviewer for a business card. This will help you remember with whom you spoke. Also, send a thank-you note to the interviewer to thank him or her for taking the time to meet with you.

The Campus Visit

You will base your choice of college or university on the academic program and available support services, right? That is really only partly true. All prospective college students also base their choices on emotional reasons. They choose a college because they like it.

Like all prospective college students, you will need to visit the campus to find out if you will feel comfortable in the environment a college or university offers. You may love the hustle and bustle of a large university. Or you may prefer the more homey feel of a small-town college. You may want to be away from the city in a rural setting. Or you may choose a city campus, right in the middle of the action. Take a walk in neighboring areas outside the campus. Take pictures during your visit.

Find out how the students live. Visit a dormitory and see how rooms are set up. Eat at the dining hall. Find out where students hang out and spend some time there. Visit a fraternity or sorority house if these groups interest you. Weigh this information along with the college's academic strengths when you make your final decision. Feeling comfortable on campus will help you to feel more confident in your choice.

When you make the arrangements for your visit, ask to spend some time with a current student who uses the college's academic support services, preferably a dyslexic student. Ask this student how well the services meet his or her needs. Find out if professors are responsive to the special needs of students. Are accommodations accepted and arranged easily? If professors are uncooperative, will your adviser negotiate for you? Talk to this student about the accommodations you think that you will need. Find out if he or she thinks those accommodations will be available.

You can also get a feel for the social climate of the college or university from this student. Does he or she feel accepted by the other students? Is there a campus support or study group for students with special needs? How does he or she fit into the campus social scene?

Landmark College

Landmark College in Putney, Vermont, is the only fully accredited college in the United States designed for students with dyslexia and other learning disabilities. In addition to taking academic courses, students at Landmark are taught skills and strategies to take control of their learning. Landmark students do not work around their dyslexia by having other students take notes for them, by taking exams orally, or by using taped textbooks. Instead, they are taught how to learn.

Unlike a conventional college or university, students at Landmark receive more individual attention. Classes are small, averaging seven students. The student-faculty ratio is three to one. Landmark offers an associate's degree in general studies. This degree is the equivalent of a similar degree from a conventional two-year junior college. The goal of Landmark's program is to provide a solid foundation for success when students move on to a four-year college or university. Noncredit courses teach study skills, written and oral expression, critical thinking, and listening comprehension. Credit courses offer college-level material with enough flexibility to allow students to follow their academic interests. Before graduation, students receive guidance from the office of college placement and career preparation. About 80 percent of Landmark graduates go on to four-year colleges, while many others enter the workplace directly.

College Learning
Strategies

You have been accepted to college. Now what should you do? Most colleges and universities have guidelines and procedures to help learning disabled students succeed. Special accommodations, including tutors, lower course loads, extended time on tests, or note-takers in class may be available to you. Remember that you must be an advocate for yourself. It is up to you to determine what help you will need and to find out how to get it.

Begin by analyzing yourself. What are your strengths? Where do you need the most help? Can you listen to a lecture and take notes at the same time? Will you need extra time to finish in-class assignments? Do you need audio-recorded textbooks? Do you need tutoring before the semester starts to improve your basic math or language skills? Can you organize your time and stick to your schedule? A good understanding of your own needs will make your college experience more successful.

Many of the skills you will need work well for all college students. Procrastination—putting off until tomorrow what you should be doing today—will be your worst enemy. Waiting until the last minute greatly increases your level of stress. Two key ideas will help you: Whenever possible, work ahead; and schedule and organize carefully.

Most college professors are required to provide a syllabus to their students during the first week of class. The syllabus will tell you the titles of textbooks, the dates assignments are due, and the dates of tests and exams. In many cases, however, the professor will be able to give you some of this information before the semester begins. You may be able to begin reading during the summer or over a winter or spring break. For example, most English professors know which books will be required reading. Ask your professor for the reading list so that you can begin before the semester starts. Many classic novels and plays are also available as books on tape. You should be able to find many of them in your school or public library

Scheduling has two parts: scheduling your classes and scheduling your time. In order to avoid overloading yourself, take different kinds of classes during a semester. Try not to take too many classes that require a lot of reading and writing at the same time. Mix English or history with art or music. Find out which electives, the courses you are allowed to choose, will not require a heavy load of reading and writing, and consider taking those.

College gives you some course scheduling options that are not available in high school. First, you may decide to drop a course that becomes a problem. If you receive low grades early in the semester, dropping the course may be the best option. One difficult course can affect your grades for the entire semester. Your struggle may drain valuable time from the courses in which you could be more successful. Be careful, though, to watch for the deadline to drop the course without penalty. Also, be sure that you do not drop more than the minimum number of credits required to continue as a full-time student.

The second option is the ability to ask for an incomplete. By talking to your professor, you may be able to arrange to extend the deadline to turn in assignments beyond the end of the regular semester. Usually, the maximum extension runs until the beginning of the next semester. Your grade report will indicate "incomplete" until the requirements are met. You must complete all assignments to receive a grade in the class.

Once you have your courses arranged, schedule your time carefully. Do your best to stick to your schedule. Use a daily planner that lists each hour of each day. When you have a syllabus for each course, write in the dates that assignments are due and tests or exams are given. Block out time to study, with extra time just before tests. Break large projects or papers into smaller tasks and block out time for them. For example, schedule time for research, organization of information, outlining, writing the draft, and editing.

Do not forget to schedule time for fun. Yes, you may need to spend more time on your studies than your friends do. But give yourself a chance to relax and kick back a bit.

During the semester, keep in close communication with your professors. Explain your dyslexia to them. Discuss how you will work together toward your success. Do your best to create a partnership with your professors. You will also probably be assigned an academic advisor. Explain your needs to your advisor and keep him or her informed as well.

Most professors want their students to be successful and are willing to make accommodations to help them. You should understand that this will most likely create additional work for your professors. Make it obvious that you appreciate their efforts.

Most of all, be sure you do your part by being prepared for class. Do your best to attend every class. Use resources provided by the university that do not involve your professors. Services such as writing labs and tutoring programs will also be very valuable to you.

Most college campuses have writing labs. This service usually provides student mentors who will review and discuss your paper with you. Your mentor will be available through all steps of the writing process. You may want to bring your assignment to the writing lab right away. Your mentor can help steer your research in the right direction. Mentors can also provide help with organizing your information. Most important, they will read your draft. They will help you to recognize grammatical errors and to organize your thoughts more clearly.

Many writing labs also have computers. Sometimes computers are located in another room designated as the computer lab. Writing on a computer will be very helpful for you. First, because you may have dysgraphia, or handwriting difficulties, you will want your mentor or tutor to be able to read your draft. Also, the spelling and grammar checking tools of most word-processing programs will pick up many of your errors. It will be dangerous to rely too heavily on these tools, however. Spell checkers will recognize words that are spelled incorrectly but not those that are used incorrectly—for example, *to* and *too* or *their* and *there*.

Find out about the university's tutoring program and use

it. Many tutoring programs do not have enough tutors to fill all their requests. You will be competing with all students, not just those with special needs. Try to get on the schedule even before the semester starts. Do not wait until your grades are a problem to seek help.

After you have investigated all the programs your university offers to its students, work with your professors and your adviser to fill in the gaps. You may be provided with a note-taker if you need one. If one is not available, talk to your professor about using a tape recorder in class to record lectures. Do not rely on your recorder too heavily, however. Batteries can wear down. Tapes can break. If the tape recorder stops working in the middle of an important lecture, you may find yourself in serious trouble. Keep an extra supply of batteries and tapes with you, just in case.

You may be able to ask another student to help you with note taking. You can ask to photocopy another student's notes. Always organize your notes immediately after class. Having written notes is a good backup to your tape-recorded lecture.

Find other people who will be able to help you. When writing papers, ask to submit an early draft to your professor. If your professor is unavailable, you may ask for this kind of help from a teaching assistant. Teaching assistants are often found in large universities with graduate schools. They usually receive a tuition reduction in exchange for assisting professors who teach undergraduate courses. If neither your professor nor a teaching assistant is available, another student in your course may be willing to help you. At the very least, always have someone—a parent, sibling, or friend—read your paper before you turn it in.

Also, use other people to help you study for a test. Study with a classmate or two if possible. Talking out loud about your questions should help you understand and organize your information.

As you work through the semester, you may have trouble taking written exams even though you have studied and attended all the classes. If this problem continues, talk to your professor or academic adviser about arranging to have oral exams instead. Perhaps you could work on a special project rather than taking the exam.

Be sure to show your appreciation to your professors, friends, mentors, and advisers. The extra help they give you also creates extra work for them. Make it very clear that you are working hard, too, and are earning their support.

Working Toward a Career

Not everyone who graduates from high school will go on to college. But almost everyone, even those who do go to college, will eventually need a job. The feeling of satisfaction that comes from a job well done increases self-esteem. When you work hard, you earn the rewards that result. Fortunately, exams and term papers are usually not part of the working world.

A successful transition to the world of work requires careful planning. Like students who are planning to attend college, you will need to take a close look at yourself. What are your strengths and weaknesses? How can those weaknesses be improved? What are your interests? Once you understand yourself, you can better match your skills and interests with a career that will be satisfying for you.

The National Information Center for Children and Youth with Disabilities recommends a structured program to help you reach your career goals. Beginning as early as junior high school, you should begin thinking about careers. There are so many! The best way to find out about them is to talk to as many different people as possible. Yes, this means that you will need to talk to adults. But you will find that most people are very happy to talk about themselves and what they do. They may even invite you to spend a day with them on the job.

Many high schools hold career fairs. Representatives from different fields will visit your school to talk about what they do. They will also tell you what training they needed for their jobs. Your school may also invite individuals to talk about their jobs. Take advantage of these opportunities. The more information you collect about careers, the more options you will give yourself.

You need to begin planning as early as possible. Early planning will help you choose your high school courses to help you prepare for different careers. Your high school may offer technical or vocational courses that give you real training for your career.

It may be difficult for you to fit a part-time job into your schedule during the school year. But try to get some work experience during the summer. Even volunteering can give you valuable experience.

To be successful in the workplace, everyone needs basic skills. You must be able to communicate in writing well enough to write letters, memos, or reports. You should know basic arithmetic. You must be able to understand and follow verbal instructions. And you must be able to speak clearly. You may need to spend extra time strengthening these skills.

By law, an employer may not deny you a job simply because you are dyslexic. However, an employer can deny you a job that you are not qualified to perform. You must know that you can perform the job effectively in spite of your dyslexia. The best way to feel confident in your ability is to plan and prepare well.

You will need a résumé to apply for a job. Your résumé will describe your job objective and your education and work experience. You may also include awards or special achievements and extracurricular activities. Your counselor probably has sample résumés that you can use as models. If not, many books are available on résumé writing.

The Rehabilitation Act of 1973 and the Americans with Disabilities Act are federal laws that prohibit discrimination based on disability or handicap as long as the employee is able to perform the job. The Rehabilitation Act applies only to employers who receive federal financial assistance. The Americans with Disabilities Act has a broader scope. It also covers private employers as long as they employ fifteen or more people. According to these laws, you must show that you are "otherwise qualified, with or without reasonable accommodations, for the job, promotion or employment benefit being sought." Accommodations are considered reasonable when they do not create "undue hardship" for the employer. For example, changing the job or reassigning some of the required tasks to other employees may be considered undue hardship. Providing a telephone amplifying device for an employee who is hard of hearing would not be considered undue hardship. Asking a supervisor to give you spoken, in place of written, instructions should also not be considered undue hardship.

Before a job interview, you should decide whether to disclose your dyslexia. Being up front may be the best approach. Your employer may appreciate your honesty and be more open to discussing minor accommodations. Keeping your dyslexia a secret until after you are on the job may cause unnecessary resentment later.

During an interview, employers are not allowed to ask

if you have a learning disability. They also may not ask about your reading or math skills, or whether you received special education services in high school. Their questions should relate only to the job, your ability to work with other people, and your ability to work within the company's schedule.

Rejection is part of the job search process. Try not to be too discouraged. Few people, dyslexic or not, walk out of their first interview with the job of their dreams. Patience and persistence may prove to be your most important job search skills.

Preparing for a Job Interview

Jim wanted to work in sales. He liked being with people. He enjoyed working with customers to help them find the perfect gift. During the last two summers, he had spent time working at a pretzel stand at the mall. He knew that was not the kind of sales job that would become a real career. But he hoped that his experience there would help him get the job he was interviewing for.

Jim was applying for a job as a salesman in Monroe Brothers Men's Clothing Store. If he got the job, he would work on commission to sell men's suits, clothing, and accessories.

The more you prepare for a job interview, the more confident you will feel during the interview. Find out as much information as you can about the company where you are applying. If it is a large company, you can call and ask for a copy of the annual report. Many companies have Web sites that discuss their products and long-term goals. Mention some of the information you learn during your interview. You will impress the interviewer with your initiative.

Jim had called to arrange for an interview with the store manager. Two days before his appointment, Jim went to the store and pretended to shop. One of the salesmen saw Jim and smiled. "Is there anything I can help you with?" the salesman asked Jim.

"No, thanks," Jim said. "I am just looking."

"Fine. If you need anything, just let me know," said the salesman. "We have men's dress shirts on sale this week."

Jim watched the salesman for a while. He also noticed that he was wearing a suit and tie that looked as if they came from the store. Before he left, he asked the cashier for a copy of the job application form. He planned to fill it out at home and bring it with him to the interview.

Before you go to the interview, think of some questions you might be asked and prepare the answers. Expect to discuss your reasons for applying for this job at this company. Be specific. Many books are available to help you through the job interview process. Most of the suggestions will apply to dyslexic applicants as well as nondyslexics.

On the day of the interview, Jim arrived at the store ten minutes early. He was wearing a gray pinstriped suit that he had borrowed from his cousin, Rich. He had on his dad's tie. The store manager, Mr. Greene, came out of his office and shook Jim's hand.

"How are you today?" asked Mr. Greene.

"Fine, thank you" said Jim. "My name is Jim Sullivan. I am applying for the job as salesman."

"Yes, please come with me," said Mr. Greene. He led Jim back into his office.

"Sit down, Jim, and tell me why you want to work at Monroe Brothers."

"I like your clothes," said Jim. "You give your customers plenty of style, but your prices are not too expensive. The suits are of good quality. You also do alterations for free, which I think would be a good selling point."

"Have you worked in sales before?" asked Mr. Greene.

"I worked at the pretzel stand in the mall," said Jim. "I know that is not the same kind of sales, but I had to please my customers and keep the cash register balanced. Sometimes, especially in the summer, we had long lines and people became very impatient. I had to keep my cool and smile even when customers were rude. I think my experience there will help me handle customers with a smile at Monroe's, too."

Practice interviewing with a friend or parent. Look the interviewer straight in the eye and answer as clearly as possible. You should also have some questions for the interviewer. It is a good idea to bring some notes to help you remember your questions. Even if you have sent a copy of your résumé to the company, bring an extra one with you. If filling out application forms is a problem for you, call and ask that a copy be sent to you. Fill it out ahead of time, ask someone to proofread it, and bring it with you.

Mr. Greene and Jim talked for a while longer.
Jim had decided to tell Mr. Greene about his dyslexia. He knew he could do the job. He thought it

would be easier to convince Mr. Greene to give him a try if he was honest right from the beginning.

"Before I go, Mr. Greene, I want to tell you that I am dyslexic," said Jim. "That means that sometimes I read very slowly. I also have pretty poor handwriting. But I am very careful. I may need to ask the cashier to check my sales slips."

"Thanks for being honest," said Mr. Greene. "Honesty is very important to me—more important than how fast you can read. If you are willing to work evenings and weekends, you can start next Monday."

Before the interview, make sure that you know how to get to the company. Know the names and titles of the people with whom you will be speaking. Understand what kind of clothing is appropriate. Do employees dress casually or more formally? You can ask this on the phone. Be sure to dress like the employees. On the day of the interview, leave extra time to be sure you arrive early. You will be nervous. Anyone interviewing for a job usually is. Try your best to be positive and confident.

After the interview, make some notes or record your impressions of the interview and the company. Send a thank-you letter to the interviewer. Thank him or her for taking the time to talk to you and express again your interest in the job.

Accommodations on the Job

Jim had been working at Monroe Brothers for two weeks. He was doing very well. He sold two suits the first Saturday that he worked! But his dyslexia had caused some confusion. Sometimes, when he was figuring out the price, he reversed the numbers. Mr. Greene had asked to meet with him.

"Come in and sit down, Jim," said Mr. Greene. "You are doing a great job on the sales floor. The other salesmen like working with you. Our customers are happy, which, of course, is very important. But twice this week, we have had difficulty balancing the books at the end of the day because you reversed numbers on your sales slip. I would like to find a way to stop that from happening. Do you have any suggestions?"

"Yes," said Jim. "I would like to bring a small tape recorder to the store. You know, the kind that newspaper reporters use. I can 'talk' my sales slip into the tape recorder."

"That is a good idea," said Mr. Greene. "We will give that a try."

Whether you talk about job accommodations during your interview or wait until you are on the job is up to you. Your employer is required to provide reasonable accommodations that do not cause him or her undue hardship.

Before you apply for a job, you should be reasonably sure that you are able to perform the duties it requires. A simple change in procedure, however, may make it much easier for you to do your job effectively.

If you have difficulty reading written instructions, perhaps a coworker could read them for you. If your company has voice mail, perhaps your supervisor could record the instructions there. If you have difficulty working in an open space with lots of distractions, perhaps you could take your work into a quiet office or a conference room that is not being used. These kinds of accommodations should not cause undue hardship to your supervisor or coworkers.

Famous Dyslexics

Many famous inventors are believed to have had learning disabilities. Thomas Edison, Albert Einstein, Alexander Graham Bell, and Leonardo da Vinci are among them. It is possible that the special way their brains worked helped to increase their creativity. When these men lived, however, learning disabilities and dyslexia had not been diagnosed.

The following celebrities, athletes, politicians, and successful businesspeople have all succeeded while struggling with dyslexia.

Nolan Ryan, Hall of Fame Pitcher

On July 12, 1989, at the age of forty-two, Nolan Ryan became the oldest pitcher to win an All-Star Game. He holds the major league record for strikeouts—5,714. In one season, in 1973, he struck out 383 batters. Ricky Henderson said, "If you haven't been struck out by Nolan Ryan, you're nobody."

When he was in elementary school, Nolan Ryan sometimes felt like a nobody. He struggled in the classroom. Most of the time he felt stupid. His dyslexia was not discovered until he was an adult.

Nolan met his wife, Ruth, while they were in high school. She remembers his difficulty. "One teacher thought he was stupid and wanted to fail him," Ruth said. "He was a C student, with a couple of D's and F's mixed in. The hardest thing for him was spelling."

By the time he was a junior, Nolan was burning baseballs over home plate. When he graduated from high school, he was signed by the Mets.

John Chambers, Chief Executive Officer, Cisco Systems

When John Chambers was in elementary school, he was laughed at by his classmates for being a slow learner. Because of his dyslexia, he dislikes reading and never does it for pleasure. But he compensates for his reading difficulties with an amazing memory. He remembers almost everything he hears. When he gives speeches, he talks without notes.

John received a law degree from West Virginia University and an MBA from Indiana University. In 1999, Cisco Systems, a large computer hardware and software manufacturer, was chosen the third best company to work for by *Fortune* magazine. Over 20,000 people work for Cisco around the world.

Paul Orfalea, President of Kinko's

When Paul Orfalea was in college, he rented a small garage near campus and began selling notebooks, pens, and pencils to his fellow students. He also had a photocopier and offered copying services. Some days he made $1,000. He sent his workers into the college dorms, selling door-to-door. He listened to the needs of his customers and the suggestions of his coworkers. He called his business Kinko's from the nickname his friends gave him because of his curly hair. There are now more than 800 Kinko's stores worldwide.

Paul's dyslexia was not discovered until he was in eighth grade. Before that, he had his eyes tested, had speech therapy, and spent his summers in remedial classes. Fortunately, his parents kept searching for the real reason for his inability to read. Finally, his dyslexia was diagnosed. He began to receive special instruction in phonetics. He was able to get by in reading but continued to be a very poor speller.

Now he likes to talk to college and high school students about succeeding in spite of a disability. "I tell them to work with their strengths, not their weaknesses," he said.

Neil Bush

When President George Bush and First Lady Barbara Bush moved into the White House in 1989, their children were grown. The Bushes had seen their sons and daughter through birthday parties, Little League, and trips to the doctor.

It was when her son Neil was ill with chicken pox that Barbara first became concerned about his reading skills. Neil was about six years old. "I asked him to read to me," she wrote in her memoir. "I discovered that not only could Neil not read, he didn't have a clue." Barbara was confused because Neil was getting all A's in school, including in reading. She visited Neil's classroom to find out how this could be happening. "It was a fascinating study in manipulation," she wrote. "The teacher had the children read a line or two, and when she got to Neil, he flashed that great smile of his and paused. A student helped him with the first word, the teacher the next, and so it went. Neil had been faking his way through reading—not uncommon for children with reading problems—and nobody had noticed."

Neil Bush was diagnosed with dyslexia and enrolled in a school with a reading teacher who was able to help him. Neil always had to work very hard. Barbara spent hours helping him to read. "But thanks to wonderful teachers, and a little boy who refused to give up, Neil eventually earned his undergraduate and master's degrees in business administration from Tulane University," she wrote.

Woodrow Wilson

As a child, Woodrow was a slow learner. He could not recite the alphabet until he was nine years old. He was eleven before he learned to read well. Although today's historians believe that Woodrow must have been dyslexic, at the time learning disabilities were not diagnosed.

Woodrow's parents were embarrassed about his slowness in school. Since no one understood his difficulties, he had to learn to overcome them on his own. According to the biography *Woodrow Wilson* by J. Perry Leavell Jr.,

Woodrow "developed strong powers of concentration and a near-photographic memory. When he was sixteen, he taught himself shorthand as a way of compensating for his poor handwriting." Soon after the typewriter was invented, Woodrow bought one and became a skilled typist. "Wilson's struggle with his learning handicap must have caused him pain," wrote Leavell, "but probably also contributed to his strong personality and character." These strengths would support him through the challenges of leading the United States as president during World War I. In December of 1920, Woodrow Wilson was awarded the Nobel Peace Prize.

Whoopi Goldberg

In 1990, Whoopi Goldberg won a Golden Globe Award and an Oscar as Best Supporting Actress for her role in *Ghost*. As a successful actress and comedian, she was at the top of her career. But getting there had been a long struggle.

Her problems began in high school. Whoopi could not read. "When she tried to read, the letters did not connect into words," wrote Mary Agnes Adams in *Whoopi Goldberg: From Street to Stardom*. Officials at her school labeled Whoopi "retarded." When she was seventeen, she dropped out of school.

But she turned her life around. She appeared in a one-woman show on Broadway. Steven Spielberg saw her performance and cast her in *The Color Purple* in 1985. She won a Golden Globe Award and an Oscar nomination for her performance. She appeared on television as

Guinan in *Star Trek: The Next Generation* and hosted her own talk show. Whoopi Goldberg has appeared in over fifty films.

Tom Cruise

Dyslexia often runs in families. When Tom Cruise began having trouble in school, his mother, Mary Lee, knew what to do. She is also dyslexic, and so are Tom's three sisters.

For a while, Tom's teachers did not recognize his dyslexia. Tom and his family moved often, making it hard for teachers to keep track of his progress. Some just thought he was dumb. Others were not sure how to help him. "Tom's dyslexia made it difficult for him to deal with his schoolwork," wrote Jolene M. Anthony in *Tom Cruise.* "Letters would magically switch themselves around and entire words and sentences appeared fractured and backward."

Tom's mother helped him and his sisters, checking their homework. Because of his hard work, Tom is now able to read for pleasure. He has starred in over twenty movies, including *A Few Good Men, Top Gun,* and *Mission Impossible.* In 1990, he was nominated for an Oscar as Best Actor for his role in *Born on the Fourth of July.* He was nominated again in 1997 for *Jerry Maguire,* and in 2000 for *Magnolia.*

In 1985, Tom received an award for Outstanding Learning Disabled Achievement. Five others, including Cher, athlete Bruce Jenner, artist Robert Rauschenberg, and businessmen Richard C. Strauss and G. Chris Anderson, also received the award.

Cher

Cher did not realize that she was dyslexic until her daughter, Chastity, began having problems in school. When Chastity was tested and diagnosed as dyslexic, Cher finally understood her own struggles.

During her school years, her family and her teachers thought Cher was lazy. She knew that she was trying hard. Her frustrations caused her to become a discipline problem. Finally, at age sixteen, she dropped out of school for good.

Today, knowing the cause of her problem does not mean it has disappeared. "Cher is still a very poor reader," wrote J. Randy Taraborrelli in *Cher: A Biography*. "Writing out a check was extremely difficult for a long time (thank goodness for charge cards). Scripts are especially hard work. When she has a new part for a movie or TV show, she learns it very slowly. She often memorizes some of her lines the first time she reads the script." Even simple tasks, like dialing a phone, can be very difficult.

Cher met Sonny Bono in 1964 when she was sixteen years old. By 1965, Sonny and Cher had begun their singing career, releasing their first hit, "I Got You Babe." They moved their act to television when *The Sonny and Cher Comedy Hour* began in 1971. Cher made her acting debut in 1983 in *Silkwood* and won an Oscar for her performance. She won her second Oscar in 1987 for her starring role in *Moonstruck*.

Conclusion

That is what learning is. You suddenly understand something you've understood all your life, but in a new way.

Doris Lessing, writer

You were born with dyslexia, and it will not go away. You know that dyslexia does not mean you are less intelligent than other people. You know that you can learn. But you may need to begin learning in a new way.

Do not expect less of yourself because you are dyslexic. Become a self-advocate. Make partners of your parents, teachers, and counselors, working together for your learning success. Learning will not be easy. Work hard. Do not give up.

Glossary

assistive technology A piece of equipment or a computer program that can help someone with a disability work around their differences.

compensatory skills Skills that help dyslexics work around, or compensate for, their learning disability.

dysgraphia A learning disability that is characterized by a great struggle with handwriting. The letters written by dysgraphics are often small, cramped, and seem to "wander" across the page.

homonyms Words that sound the same but are spelled differently.

Individual Education Program (IEP) A written agreement between a student and his or her school to determine the special education services the school will provide. An IEP also outlines educational goals and expectations for the student's future achievement.

mainstream courses Courses open to all students.

mentor An experienced peer, like a fellow college or high-school student, who guides other students.

morphology The study of how syllables join to form words.

multisensory learning A method of teaching first used by Dr. Samuel Orton. Students associate the physical act of writing with sound and letter patterns.

optical character recognition systems (OCRS)   Reading computers that take scanned text and "read" it out loud using a synthesized voice.

phonology   The study of sounds and how they work.

semantics   The meaning of language as a whole.

syntax   How the order of words creates meaning.

Where to Go for Help

In the United States

Association on Higher Education and Disability
University of Massachusetts at Boston
100 Morrissey Boulevard
Boston, MA 02125-3393
(617) 287-3880
Web site: http://www.ahead.org

Davis Dyslexia Association International
1601 Old Bayshore Highway, Suite 245
Burlingame, CA 94010
(888) 999-3324
Web site: http://www.dyslexia.com

Hello Friend: The Ennis William Cosby Foundation
P.O. Box 4061
Santa Monica, CA 90411
Web site: http://www.hellofriend.com

International Dyslexia Association
8600 Lasalle Road, Chester Building, Suite 382
Baltimore, MD 21286-2044
(800) ABC-D123
Web site: http://www.interdys.org

Landmark College
RR 1, Box 1000
Putney, VT 05346
(802) 387-4767
Web site: http://www.landmarkcollege.org

LD Resources On-line
Web site: http://www.ldresources.com

The Medical Dyslexia and ADD Treatment Center
600 Northern Boulevard
Great Neck, NY 11021
(800) 334-READ
Web site: http://www.dyslexiaonline.com

Schwab Foundation for Learning
1650 South Amphlett Boulevard, Suite 300
San Mateo, CA 94402
(800) 230-0988
Web site: http://www.schwablearning.org

In Canada

Eaton Coull Learning Group
3541 West 16th Avenue
Vancouver, BC V6R 3C2
(800) 933-4063
Web site: http://www.eclg.com

Learning Disabilities Association of Canada
323 Chapel Street
Ottawa, ON KIN7Z2
(613) 238-5721
Web site: http://www.educ.queensu.ca/~lda

Summer Camp Directories

Directory of Summer Camps for Children with Learning Disabilities
Learning Disabilities Association
4156 Library Road
Pittsburgh, PA 15234
(412) 341-1515

Association of Independent Camps
Web site: http://www.intercamp.com

Kids' Camps
5455 North Federal Highway, Suite O
Boca Raton, FL 33487
Web site: http://www.kidscamps.com

Special Testing Accommodations

ACT
P.O. Box 4028
Iowa City, IA 52243-4028

SAT
Services for Students with Disabilities
P.O. Box 6226
Princeton, NJ 08541-6226
Web site: http://www.ets.org

Alliance for Technology Access
2173 East Francisco Boulevard
San Rafael, CA 94901
(800) 455-7970
Web site: http://www.ataccess.org

Center for Applied Special Technology (CAST)
39 Cross Street
Peabody, MA 01960
(508) 531-8555
Web site: http://www.cast.org

Recordings for the Blind and Dyslexic
20 Roszel Road
Princeton, NJ 08540
(800) 221-4792
Web site: http://www.rfbd.org

For Further Reading

General Resources

Cronin, Eileen M. *Helping Your Dyslexic Child*. Rocklin, CA: Prima Publishing, 1997.

Davis, Ronald D. *The Gift of Dyslexia*. New York: Penguin Putnam, 1994 (also available on audiotape).

Hurford, Daphne M. *To Read or Not to Read: Answers to All Your Questions About Dyslexia*. New York: Scribner, 1998.

Snowling, Margaret. *Dyslexia: A Cognitive Developmental Perspective*. Cambridge, MA: Blackwell Publishers,1987.

Fiction

Betancourt, Jeanne. *My Name Is Brain*. New York: Scholastic, 1993.

Griffith, Joe. *How Dyslexic Benny Became a Star*. Dallas, TX: Yorktown Press, 1998.

Janover, Caroline. *Josh: A Boy with Dyslexia*. Burlington VT: Waterfront Books, 1988.

Janover, Caroline. *The Worst Speller in Jr. High*. Minneapolis, MN: Free Spirit, 1995.

Polacco, Patricia. *Thank You, Mr. Falker*. New York: Philomel, 1998.

Educational Resources

Lewis, Erica Lee. *Help Yourself: Handbook for College-Bound Students with Learning Disabilities.* New York: Princeton Review, 1996.

Nadeau, Kathleen. *Survival Guide for College Students with ADD or LD.* New York: Magination Press, 1994.

Koehler, Michael and Marybeth Kravets. *Counseling Secondary Students with Learning Disabilities: A Ready-to-Use Guide to Help Students Prepare for College and Work.* West Nyack, NY: Center for Applied Research in Education, 1998.

Mangrum. Charles, and Stephen Strichart. *Peterson's Guide to Colleges with Programs for Learning Disabled Students.* Lawrenceville, NJ: Peterson's Guides, 1997.

Video

Transitions to Postsecondary Learning

Video and booklets for students with learning disabilities and/or attention deficit/hyperactivity disorder. Available from Eaton Coull Learning Group (800) 933-4063.

Index